PRAISE FOR *THE MONK WHO SOLD HIS FERRARI*

"Nothing less than sensational. This book will bless your life."

Mark Victor Hansen, co-author, *Chicken Soup for the Soul*

"A captivating story that teaches as it delights."

Paulo Coelho, author of *The Alchemist*

"This is a fun, fascinating, fanciful adventure into the realms of personal development, personal effectiveness and individual happiness. It contains treasures of wisdom that can enrich and enhance the life of every single person."

Brian Tracy, author of *Maximum Achievement*

"Robin S. Sharma has an important message for all of us — one that can change our lives. He's written a one-of-a-kind handbook for personal fulfillment in a hectic age."

Scott DeGarmo, past publisher, *Success Magazine*

"Robin Sharma has created an enchanting tale that incorporates the classic tools of transformation into a simple philosophy of living. A delightful book that will change your life."

Elaine St. James, author of *Simplify Your Life* and *Inner Simplicity*

". . . sheds light on life's big questions."

The Edmonton Journal

"*The Monk Who Sold His Ferrari* is coherent, useful and definitely worth reading . . . It can truly help readers cope with the rat race."

The Kingston Whig-Standard

"A magnificent book. Robin S. Sharma is the next Og Mandino."

Dottie Walters, author of *Speak & Grow Rich*

". . . simple wisdom that anyone can benefit from."

The Calgary Herald

"This book could be classified as *The Wealthy Barber* of personal development . . . [It contains] insightful messages on the key concepts which help bring greater balance, control and effectiveness in our daily lives."

Investment Executive

". . . a treasure — an elegant and powerful formula for true success and happiness. Robin S. Sharma has captured the wisdom of the ages and made it relevant for these turbulent times. I couldn't put it down."

Joe Tye, author of *Never Fear, Never Quit*

". . . simple rules for reaching one's potential."

The Halifax Daily News

"A wonderful story sharing lessons that can enrich your life."

Ken Vegotsky, author of *The Ultimate Power*

"Sharma guides readers toward enlightenment."

The Chronicle-Herald

"A wonderfully crafted parable revealing a set of simple yet surprisingly potent ideas for improving the quality of anyone's life. I'm recommending this gem of a book to all of my clients."

George Williams, president, Karat Consulting International

"Robin Sharma offers personal fulfillment along the spiritual highroad."

The Ottawa Citizen

Leadership Wisdom from The Monk Who Sold His Ferrari

The 8 Rituals of Visionary Leaders

Robin S. Sharma, LL.B., LL.M.

HarperCollins*Publishers*Ltd

http://www.harpercollins.com/canada

HarperCollins books may be purchased for educational, business, or sales promotional
use. For information please write: Special Markets Department, HarperCollins Canada,
55 Avenue Road, Suite 2900, Toronto, Ontario M5R 3L2.

Text design: Karen Petherick

First edition

Canadian Cataloguing in Publication Data

Sharma, Robin Shilp, 1964-
Leadership wisdom from the monk who sold his Ferrari : the 8 rituals of visionary leaders

ISBN 0-00-2255722-3 (bound)
ISBN 0-00-638562-1 (pbk.)

1. Leadership. I. Title.

PR6054.I26B37 1996   823'.914   C95-932438-0

96 97 98 99 WEB 10 9 8 7 6 5 4 3 2 1

Printed and bound in Canada by Webcom

To my daughter, Bianca. May you always be
the model of joy.

To the many readers of *The Monk Who Sold His Ferrari*
who took the time out of their busy lives to tell
me how this simple book touched them.
You have moved me.

And to all those leaders who deeply honor the
sacred trust between them and the people they have the
privilege to lead. Keep blessing lives and liberating talent.

❦

This is the true joy in life, being used for a purpose recognized by yourself as a mighty one, being a true force of Nature instead of a feverish little clod of ailments and grievances complaining that the world will not devote itself to making you happy. . . . I want to be thoroughly used up when I die. For the harder I work, the more I live. I rejoice in life for its own sake. Life is no brief candle to me. It's a sort of splendid torch which I've got to hold up for the moment and I want to make it burn as brightly as possible before handing it on to future generations.

George Bernard Shaw

CONTENTS

ACKNOWLEDGMENTS

To the many thousands of people who read *The Monk Who Sold His Ferrari*, were inspired by its lessons and shared its wisdom with their families and friends. Thank you for helping me spread this message for life improvement.

To all who attended my public and corporate seminars across the United States and Canada. Special thanks to Sharma Leadership International's corporate clients who sponsored personal and organizational leadership programs for their employees. I feel privileged to be able to contribute to your success.

To the entire team at HarperCollins. You folks have made this a most joyful and satisfying experience. Special thanks to Claude Primeau for your guidance, Iris Tupholme for your faith in me, Judy Brunsek, Tom Best, Marie Campbell, David Millar, Lloyd Kelly, Doré Potter, Valerie Applebee, Neil Erickson and Nicole Langlois, my insightful and highly competent editor.

To my valued team at Sharma Leadership International for your energy, support and for managing my nonstop corporate seminar and media schedule.

To my mom and dad. I have so very much respect, appreciation and love for you. To my dear brother, Sanjay, my tireless supporter and confidant, to his wife, Susan, to my in-laws, Satya Paul and Krishna Sharma and Sandeep, for all your kindness and encouraging words.

And to Alka, for your constant support, to my young son, Colby, for keeping me playful amid the writing of the manuscript (partly with your Curious George stories) and to my daughter, Bianca, for being a light.

❦

CHAPTER ONE

A Wild Ride to Success

It was the saddest day of my life. As I arrived at work after a rare long weekend spent hiking and laughing in the mountains with my kids, I saw two enormous security guards hunched over the mahogany desk in my coveted corner office. Running closer, I could see that they were rifling through my files and peeking into the precious documents on my laptop computer, oblivious to the fact that I had spotted them. Finally, one of them noticed me standing there, my face flushed with anger, my hands shaking at the sight of this unforgivable invasion. With an expression that revealed not a hint of emotion, he looked at me and spoke fifteen words that left me feeling as if I'd just been kicked in the chest, "Mr. Franklin, you have been fired. We must escort you out of the building immediately."

With that simple dispatch, I went from being the senior vice-president of the fastest-growing software company on the continent to a man without a future. And believe me, I took my dismissal very hard. Failure was a foreign concept to me, an experience I had no idea how to manage. In college, I'd been a golden boy, the kid with the perfect grades, the beautiful girls and the boundless future. I made the varsity track team, was elected class president and even found the time to host a hugely popular jazz show on our campus radio station. It seemed to all concerned I was gifted and destined for great success. One day I'd overheard one of my old professors saying to a colleague, "If I had the chance to live my life over again, I'd like to come back as Peter Franklin."

Mind you, my talents were not as natural as everyone believed. The true source of my achievements could be traced back to a punishing work ethic and an almost obsessive desire to win. My father had come to this country as a penniless immigrant many years ago with a deeply held vision of a more tranquil, prosperous and happy life for his young family. He changed our family name, settled us into a three-room apartment in the honest part of town and started working tirelessly as a factory worker for minimum wage, a job he would keep for the next forty years of his life. And though he had no formal education, I'd never met a wiser man — until recently, when I met a most extraordinary human being, a person who you truly must get to know. I promise to tell you more about him shortly. You will never be the same.

My father's dream for me was a simple one: get a first-class education at a first-class school. A career of peak achievement and just compensation would then be assured, or so he thought. His firm belief was that a well-developed base of personal knowledge laid the foundation for a successful life. "No matter whatever happens to you, Peter, no one will ever be able to take away your education. Knowledge will always be your best friend, no matter where you go or what you do," he would often say to me while finishing his supper after another grueling fourteen-hour day at the factory he devoted most of his life to. My father was quite a man.

He was also a great storyteller, one of the best. In his home country, the elders used parables to convey the wisdom of the ages to their children, so he carried this rich tradition with him to his adopted country. From the day that my mother died suddenly while making his lunch in our well-worn kitchen until the time that my brother and I entered our teenage years, my father would send us off to a dreamy sleep with a delightful story that always had a life lesson. One that particularly stands out in my mind is about an old farmer on his deathbed, who asked his three sons to gather around him. "Sons," he said, "Death is close by and I shall soon take my last breath. But before I do, I must share a secret with you. In that field behind our farmhouse, there lies a glorious treasure. Dig deep and you shall find it. You will never have to worry about money again."

Once the old man had died, the sons ran out to the field and started digging with wild abandon. They dug for many hours and continued for many days. No part of the field was left untilled as they put every ounce of their youthful energy into this task. But, alas, no treasure could be found. Eventually, they gave up, cursing their father for his apparent deception and wondering why he would choose to make such fools of them. However, the following fall, that same field yielded a harvest the likes of which the entire community had never seen before. The three sons quickly became rich. And they never worried about money again.

So, from my father, I learned the power of dedication, diligence and hard work. In my college days, I toiled day and night, eager to stay on the Dean's List and to fulfill the dreams my dad had set for me. I won scholarship after scholarship and diligently sent my aging father a small check at the end of every month, a portion of the salary I received from the part-time job that I held.

This was a simple token of thanks for all he had done. When it came time to enter the work force, I had already been offered a lucrative management position in the high-tech field, the field of my choice. The company was called Digitech Software Strategies and it was the place where everyone wanted to work.

Astonishingly successful, the pundits predicted its meteoric growth would only continue and I felt truly honored that the firm had actively recruited me to become a member of its high-flying team. Quickly accepting the post, I began working eighty-hour weeks to prove that I was worth every penny of the lofty salary I received. Little did I know that, seven years later, the very same company would humiliate me as I had never been humiliated before.

The first few years at Digitech were good ones. They really were. I made some fine friends, learned a great deal and quickly rose through the executive ranks. I became the acknowledged superstar, a young man who had a razor-sharp mind, who knew how to work hard and who showed true commitment to the company. Though I'd never really been taught how to manage and lead people, they just kept on promoting me to ever-higher positions of responsibility.

But, without a doubt, the best thing that happened to me at Digitech Software Strategies was meeting Samantha, the woman who would eventually become my wife. A bright young manager herself, she was strikingly pretty, with a formidable intellect to match. After meeting at the Christmas party, we quickly hit it off and were soon spending what little free time we had together. From day one, Samantha was my greatest fan, a true believer in my potential and talent. "Peter, you'll be the CEO," she would regularly tell me, giving me a soft smile. "I know you've got what it takes." Unfortunately, not everyone felt the same way. Or perhaps they did.

The CEO of Digitech Software ruled the company like a dictator. A self-made man with a vicious streak, he had an ego that matched his grossly inflated paycheck. When I first started working with him, he was polite though reserved. But when word started to spread about my abilities and my ambitions, he grew cold, often communicating with me through terse memos when the situation called for something less formal. Samantha called him an "insecure little clod of a man," but the fact remained that he had power. Real power. Maybe he felt that as I rose to higher management positions, I would make him look bad. Or maybe he saw too much of himself in me — and didn't like what he saw.

I have to admit, however, that I carried my own weaknesses. Foremost was a hair-trigger temper. If something went wrong at the wrong time, a rage brewed within me that I simply could not control. I have no idea where it came from, but it was there. And it was not a business asset. I'll also admit that though I think I'm a fundamentally decent person, I could be a little rough around the edges when it came to the art of managing people. Like I said, I had never received any leadership training and operated on what little instinct I had been granted. I often felt that not everyone on my team shared my work ethic and commitment to excellence, which led me to frustration. Yes, I would yell at people. Yes, I took on far more responsibility than I was capable of handling. Yes, I should have spent more time building relationships and cultivating loyalty. But there were always too many fires to put out and I never seemed to have enough time to attend to the things that needed improving. I guess I was like the mariner who spent all his time bailing water out of his boat rather than taking the time to fix the hole in it. Shortsighted at best.

And so the day came when I was fired. The months that followed were truly the darkest of my life. Thank God I had Samantha and the kids around me. They did their best to lift my spirits and encourage me to pick up the pieces of my once fast-tracked career. But those months of idleness showed me that our self-esteem is linked to our jobs. At a cocktail party, the first question we are inevitably asked is, "So what do you do for a living?" As we began our weekly round of golf, my partners would always ask, "Any news on work, Peter?" The doorman at our luxury high rise, always a master of small talk, would regularly inquire whether things were going well at the office. With no job to go to, I no longer had any answers.

I went from getting up in the morning and rushing off to the subway station, my mind full of ideas, to awakening around noon in a darkened room, littered with empty Heineken bottles, Marlboro packages and sticky Häagen-Dazs containers. I stopped reading the *Wall Street Journal* and retreated into cheesy spy novels, old western paperbacks and trashy tabloids that revealed Oprah was an alien and that Elvis was still alive, managing a McDonald's on the West Coast. I could not face reality. I just didn't want to think too hard or do too much. A numbing pain pervaded my body and resting under the covers of our four-poster bed seemed like the best place to be.

Then one day, I received a phone call. It was an old college friend who had carved out an excellent reputation as one of the best minds in the software industry. He told me that he had just quit his job as chief programmer for a large company and was getting ready to start his own firm. I still recall him telling me he had what he called "a brilliant concept" for a new line of software and needed a partner he could trust. I was his first choice. "It's a chance to build something great, Peter," he said with his usual sense of enthusiasm. "C'mon. It'll be fun."

Part of me lacked the confidence to say yes. Starting a new business is never easy, especially in the high-tech field. What if we failed? As it was, our financial situation was a mess. As senior vice-president at Digitech Software, I was paid well and lived the kind of life that my father could only have dreamed of. I drove a brand-new BMW while Samantha had her own Mercedes. The kids went to private school and spent summers at a prestigious sailing camp. My golf club's membership fees alone totalled the annual income of many of my friends. Now, with no job, the unpaid bills were piling up and many promises were being broken. It was not the ideal time to dream of my own business.

On the other hand, my wise father always told me that "nothing can defeat you unless you defeat yourself." I needed this opportunity to lift me from the darkness that had enveloped my life. I needed a reason to wake up in the morning. I needed to reconnect to that sense of passion and purpose I had felt in college when I believed that I was unstoppable and the world was truly a place of unlimited possibilities. I had enough intuition to know that life sends us gifts from time to time. Success comes to those who recognize and accept them. So I said yes.

We grandly named the company GlobalView Software Solutions and set up shop in a tiny office in a run-down industrial complex. I was CEO and my partner was the self-appointed chairman. We had no employees, no furniture and no money. But we did have a great idea. And so we started pitching our software concept to the marketplace. Fortunately, the marketplace enthusiastically responded. Soon Samantha came to work with us and we hired other employees. Our innovative software products began to sell at a phenomenal pace and our profits quickly soared. That first year of operation, *Business Success* magazine listed us as one of the country's fastest-growing companies. My father was so proud. Though he was eighty-six at the time, I still remember him carrying a huge basket of fruit into the office to celebrate our achievement. Tears streamed down his face when he looked at me and said, "Son, your mother would have been very happy today."

That was more than eleven years ago and we have continued our blistering pace of growth. GlobalView Software Solutions is now a two-billion-dollar company with 2,500 employees at eight locations around the world. Just last year we moved into our new international headquarters, a world-class complex complete with a state-of-the-art manufacturing facility, three Olympic-sized swimming pools and an amphitheater for meetings and other corporate events. My partner is no longer involved in the day-to-day operations of the company and spends most of his time on his private island in the Caribbean or mountain-climbing in Nepal. Samantha left the leadership of the company a few years ago to pursue her passion for writing and to become more involved in community service. As for me, I'm still the CEO, but now I have crushing responsibilities that consume the majority of my time. Twenty-five hundred people look to me for their livelihoods and many thousands more depend on our organization to provide products and services that help them in their daily lives.

Sadly, my father died two years after the company was formed, and though he always sensed I would be enormously successful, I don't think that even he could have imagined that we would be where we are today. I do miss him but, with all that's on my plate, I have little time to reflect on the past. I still work hard, about eighty hours on a good week. I haven't taken a real vacation in years and I'm as hard-driving, ambitious and competitive as I was the day I started work as a twenty-three-year-old kid at Digitech Software Strategies. Until I had the good fortune to meet a very special teacher a relatively short while ago, I still tried to do too much and micromanage every aspect of the business. I knew this was a weakness, but I seemed to have succeeded in spite of it.

Until that most memorable meeting, which I am about tell you about in greater detail, I still had my bad temper, a characteristic that had only worsened as the pressures on me had grown along with my business. And, despite the passage of time, I still had a hard time managing and motivating people. Oh sure, my employees listened to me. But it was not because they wanted to — it's because they had to. They had no loyalty to me and no real commitment to the company. Fear rather than respect seemed to be the reason they would carry out the commands I issued from my palatial executive suite. It seemed all my power stemmed solely from my position. And I knew that was a bad position to be in.

Let me share a little more with you about the challenges I faced as the leader of a fast-growing company in these turbulent and change-crazed times. Despite the expansion of our business, morale had plummeted. I had heard through the grapevine that some people were saying we had grown too quickly and that profits had become more important than people. Others complained that they were being forced to work too hard with not enough resources to support them. Still others complained that the tremendous change they faced on a daily basis, ranging from innovations in technology to new structures within the bureaucracy, left their heads spinning and their bodies tingling with stress. There was little trust, low productivity and even less creativity. And from what I could gather, nearly everyone in the organization believed that the blame for the problems rested squarely with one person: me. The consensus was that I just did not know how to lead.

Though GlobalView Software continued to grow, the indicators started to show that we might be headed for our first loss in many years. Although our programs still continued to sell, we were losing market share. Our people were simply not as innovative and inspired as in the early days. As a result, our products were not as well-designed and unique. To put it simply: people just didn't seem to care anymore. And I knew that if allowed to continue, that mind-set would eventually spell the end of our company.

Signs of apathy were everywhere. Offices were disorganized and people were consistently late. Christmas parties were poorly attended and teamwork was almost nonexistent. Conflict was routine and initiative poor. Even our new manufacturing facility began to show signs of disrepair and neglect, its once gleaming floors now littered with trash and grime.

Remarkably, all that has changed. GlobalView Software Solutions is a truly excellent company again. And I know we are growing to be even better. Our organization has been transformed through the application of a very special leadership formula given to me by a very special man. This simple yet extraordinarily powerful system has brought back the excitement that once pervaded the entire company, inspired our people to new heights of commitment, sent productivity soaring and caused our profits to skyrocket beyond even my wildest dreams. Our employees have become deeply loyal and dedicated to our shared vision for the future. They work as a dynamic and highly competent team. Even better, they love coming to work and I love working with them. We all know we have discovered something magical and we know we are now headed for something very big. Just last week, *Business Success* magazine featured me on the cover. The heading read simply, "The GlobalView Miracle: How One Company Grew Great."

So what is this miraculous and time-honored leadership formula that has made me the toast of the business community? Who was this wise visitor who revolutionized our organization and showed me how to become the kind of visionary leader these topsy-turvy times call for? I know with all my heart that the answers to these questions will change the way you lead as well as the way you live. The time has come for you to discover them.

❧

CHAPTER TWO

A Monk in My Rose Garden

It was a bizarre scene. Now that I reflect on it, I still cannot believe it happened. I had just come out of my regular Monday morning meeting with my managers after hearing that GlobalView's fortunes were going from bad to worse. In the meeting, one manager had informed me that some of our top programmers were thinking of going to work for a smaller company where their efforts would be more appreciated. He also said that the relationships between management and nonmanagement were growing more strained by the day. "They don't trust us anymore," he said angrily.

Another manager added, "Not only that, there's no teamwork in this place. Before we got so big, everyone would help one another. People truly cared about a job well done. In the old days, if we were under a deadline to ship out a big order, I still remember all of us would work together, sometimes late into the night. I even remember times when the programmers and managers rolled up their sleeves to help people in shipping seal boxes and get them ready for loading onto the delivery trucks. Now it's every person for himself. It's a bunker mentality. I really can't stand it anymore."

Though I remained uncharacteristically calm during the meeting, I broke into a sweat as I walked down the long hallway that linked the boardroom to my office. The tension of the past few months was killing me, and I knew I had to do something to stop the company's downward spiral. I just didn't know who to talk to or what to do. Sure, I could hire a team of consultants to offer some quick-fix solutions to the problems that plagued us. But I felt I had to dig deeper to strike at the roots of what had caused us to go from being a visionary company full of passionate and compassionate people to a bulky bureaucracy where people could not wait for closing time.

By the time I reached my office, perspiration dripped off my forehead and my shirt was soaked. My executive assistant, seeing my state, rushed toward me and grabbed my arm. As she escorted me to the plush leather couch that sat next to one of the many floor-to-ceiling bookcases in my imperial office, she asked if she should call my doctor or perhaps even an ambulance. Not even giving her the courtesy of a reply, I lay down on the couch and closed my eyes. I had read somewhere that visualizing a soothing scene in the mind's eye was a great way to calm down after a stressful encounter. And so I did my best.

Just as I began to relax, I was startled by a loud noise. It sounded as if someone had thrown a rock against one of the windows in my office. I leapt to my feet and ran to the large main window in search of the culprit. But I could see no one. Maybe the stress I had been suffering from was playing games with my imagination. As I slowly returned to the couch, it happened again, but this time even louder. 'Who could it be?' I wondered, thinking I should have my assistant call security immediately. 'Probably another disgruntled computer programmer pushing his luck with

the boss,' I thought, growing even more annoyed at the distur-
bance. I darted to the window yet another time and, this time, saw
a figure standing in the center of the sweeping rose garden that
my second-floor office overlooked. As I squinted my eyes and
looked more carefully, I was shocked by what I saw.

It was a striking young man who appeared to be wearing a
hooded red robe, the kind I'd seen the Tibetan monks wear on a
trip that I had made to that exotic land more than a decade earlier.
As the rays of the sun illuminated the handsome, unlined face of
the stranger, his robe flapped in the light wind, giving him a mysterious, almost ethereal appearance. He had a big smile on his face.
And on his feet he wore sandals.

After realizing this was not some hallucination of an over-
worked CEO whose company was slowly sliding into oblivion, I
pounded on the window in anger. The young man did not move. He
remained in a fixed position and kept smiling. Then he offered me
an enthusiastic wave. I could not stand this kind of disrespect. This
clown was trespassing on my property, spoiling my rose garden
and clearly attempting to make a fool out of me. I immediately
commanded my executive assistant, Arielle, to call security. "Have
them bring our strange visitor up to my office right now, before he
gets away," I ordered. "He needs to be taught a lesson — the likes
of which he will never forget."

Within minutes, four security guards were at my door, one of
them carefully holding the young stranger, who appeared to be
cooperating with them, by the arm. Surprisingly, the young man
was still smiling and he radiated a sense of strength and serenity
as he stood in the doorway to my office. He did not appear to be a
bit concerned about being caught by security and marched into my
office. And though he said nothing, I was also struck by the

strange feeling that I was in the presence of a man of great knowledge. I experienced the same feeling I used to have when I was with my dad. I really cannot explain it any more than that. Call it intuition, but my gut told me the young man was far wiser than his youthful face showed. Actually, I think it was his eyes that gave it away.

In my years in business, I have discovered that a person's eyes can reveal the truth. They can disclose warmth, insecurity, insincerity or integrity, if one simply takes the time to study them. The young man's eyes told me he had wisdom. They also indicated he had a passion for life and perhaps a slight mischievous streak. They seemed to sparkle when the sunlight pouring into my office caught them. Seen up close, the young man's ruby red robe was quite splendid in its texture and design. And despite being inside, he had chosen to leave the hood on, lending further mystery to his remarkable appearance.

"Who are you and why were you throwing rocks at my window?" I demanded, my face growing hot and my palms growing even more sweaty.

The young man remained silent, his full lips holding their smile. Then he started to move his hands, bringing them together in a prayer stance, offering me the traditional greeting of the people of India.

'This guy is unbelievable!' I thought. 'First he treads through my rose garden, the garden I love looking at from my office when things get crazy. Then he starts pitching rocks at my window, scaring the heck out of me. And now, when he is surrounded by four burly, no-nonsense security guards who could floor him in an instant, he plays games with me.'

"Look, kid, I don't know who you are or where you've come

from, and to be honest, I don't really care," I exclaimed. "You can keep wearing that silly robe and giving me that silly smile. Be as cocky as you like because I plan to call the police. But before I do, why don't you break that vow of silence you monks are so famous for and tell me why you are here?"

"I'm here to help you reinvent your leadership, Peter," the young man replied in a surprisingly commanding tone. "I'm here to help you get your organization back on track. And then on to world-class status."

How did he know my name? Maybe this guy was dangerous. 'I'm glad I've got security right in front of me,' I thought to myself. And what was all this nonsense about helping me "reinvent my leadership and get my company back on track?" If this clown was some kind of consultant trying to get my attention for a fat contract, he was going about it the wrong way. Why didn't he just send me a proposal like the rest of those overpriced, underworked "change agents" who have an amazing gift for creating makework projects that ensure they never miss the target dates for their early retirements.

"You have no idea who I am, do you, Peter?" he asked in a friendly tone.

"No, I'm sorry I don't. And if you don't tell me now, I'm going to kick your sorry behind down the hallway and out into the parking lot," I yelled menacingly.

"I see you still have that temper, Peter. We'll need to work on that. I'll bet it doesn't help you win the loyalty of your team. And I know it does nothing but hurt your golf game, which never was that good," said the young man, breaking into a laugh.

"Do you have any idea who you are talking to, you arrogant little troublemaker?" I screamed, disregarding the fact that the mysterious stranger was well over six feet tall and in superb physical condition. "How dare you chastise me for my temper? And how do you know so much about my golf game? If you've been following me around, I'm definitely getting the police to charge you. That's a very serious offense you know," I noted, whipping myself into a frenzy that caused me to sweat profusely once again.

Then the young man did something that astonished me. He lifted his hand and reached deep into his robe, pulling out what appeared to be a gold-plated golf ball. He then tossed it high into the air for me to catch. "I thought you might want it back," he remarked, still smiling.

I was stunned by the object now resting in the palm of my hand. For the golf ball carried an inscription: *To Julian on your fiftieth birthday, a golden golf ball for the man who has it all.* It was signed: *Your friend always, Peter.* How did the young man get this ball? I had given it to my former golfing partner, Julian Mantle, a few years ago. Julian had been a legend in the business world and one of the few friends I had been able to keep over the years. A man with an absolutely brilliant mind, he was widely acknowledged as one of the finest lawyers in the country. Unlike me, he had come from money, his grandfather being a prominent senator and his father, a highly respected judge of the Federal Court. Groomed for success at an early age, Julian graduated number one in his class at Harvard Law School and then landed a coveted position with a spectacularly successful law firm.

He rose to national prominence within a few short years, and his blue-chip client list included multibillion-dollar corporations, major sports teams and even leading governments. In his heyday, he managed a team of eighty-five talented lawyers and won a string of legal victories, which, to this day, causes me to marvel.

With an income well into the seven figures, he had everything anyone could want: a mansion in a tony neighborhood favored by celebrities, a private jet, a summer home on a tropical island and his most prized possession of all — a shiny red Ferrari parked in the center of his driveway. But, like me, Julian had his flaws.

He worked like a fiend, regularly working through the night and then catching a few hours of sleep on the couch in his princely corner office before beginning the daily grind all over again. Though I loved playing golf with him, he was hardly ever available. I mostly heard the same excuse from his executive assistant, "I'm sorry, Mr. Franklin, Mr. Mantle will not be able to join you for golf this week due to an emergency that has come up on one of his cases. He does apologize." The man pushed himself relentlessly and, over time, lost most of his friends along with his once sympathetic wife.

I honestly thought Julian had a deathwish or something. Not only did he work far too hard, he lived far too hard. He was well-known for his late-night visits to the city's finest restaurants with sexy young fashion models and for his reckless drinking escapades with a rowdy band of cronies, which often ended up in fights that were splashed across the newspapers the next day. Despite his statements to the contrary, Julian Mantle was digging himself into an early grave. I knew it, the lawyers at his firm knew it and, deep within his soul, I think he knew it.

I watched Julian's steady decline with a feeling of sadness. At the age of fifty-three, he looked as if he was in his late seventies. The constant stress and strain of his hard-driving lifestyle wreaked havoc on him physically, transforming his face into a mass of wrinkles. The late-night dinners in expensive French restaurants, smoking thick Cuban cigars and drinking cognac after cognac had left him embarrassingly overweight and he constantly complained that he was sick and tired of being sick and tired. Over time, he lost his once wicked sense of humor and rarely laughed. A time eventually came when he stopped playing golf, even though I knew he loved the sport as well as our outings together. With all the work on his plate, Julian even stopped calling me. I knew he needed my friendship as much as I welcomed his, but I guess he just didn't care.

Then tragedy struck the Great Julian Mantle. One Monday morning, in the middle of the packed courtroom where Julian was arguing a case for one of his best corporate clients, Air Atlantic, he collapsed. Amid the frenzied screams of his paralegal and the clicking cameras of the media that were present, Julian was rushed to the hospital. On arrival, he was diagnosed as having suffered a massive heart attack and was rushed into the coronary care unit. The cardiologist said Julian was as close to death as any patient he had ever seen. But somehow he survived. The doctors said Julian was a fighter and seemed to have "a heroic will to live."

That sad episode changed Julian profoundly. The very next day, he announced he was leaving the practice of law for good. I'd heard through the grapevine that Julian had headed off to India on some kind of expedition. He told one of his partners he "needed some answers" and hoped he would find them in that ancient land that had, over the centuries, gathered such great wisdom. In a striking act of closure, Julian had sold his mansion, his jet and his private island. However, it was his final gesture before departing that was his most unexpected: *Julian sold the Ferrari that he loved so much.*

My thoughts quickly returned to the young stranger in the monk's robes, now standing in the center of my office, still smiling and still wearing the hood over a thick mop of brown hair. "How did you get this gold-plated golf ball?" I asked in a quiet tone. "I gave this to a dear friend of mine a few years ago as a gift for a very special birthday."

"I know you did," replied the visitor. "And he really appreciated your gesture."

"And might I ask how you would know that?" I persisted.

"Because I'm the dear friend. I am Julian Mantle."

CHAPTER THREE

The Miraculous Transformation of a Corporate Warrior

I was astonished by what I had just heard. Could this young man in the peak of health really be Julian Mantle, a man who had fallen from the pinnacle of greatness as no one I have ever known? And if it *was* him, how could he possibly have undergone such a stunning change in appearance? I knew Julian had sold his mansion, his summer home and even given up his prized red Ferrari. I knew he'd given up the trappings of the corporate world and trekked off to the Himalayas on some fanatical mission to seek answers to the deep questions he was struggling with. But surely a simple visit to that ancient and mystical place could not have so profoundly transformed a man who had all but worked himself into the ground.

Disturbed by the bizarre scenario that had just unfolded before me, my mind began to race to some of the other possibilities. Perhaps this was a prank masterminded by one of my less-than-mature managers to inject a little levity into what was sure to be a tension-filled week? Or maybe the young man was an infiltrator from a competitor seeking to get inside our operation to see how bad things really were? Perhaps this visitor in monk's clothing was a deranged trespasser out to seriously harm me. But before I could examine these options more fully, the young man spoke.

"Peter, I know it's hard for you to believe it's really me. I'd feel exactly the same way if I were in your shoes. All I'm asking from you is a little faith, a little bit of belief in life's small miracles. There's a purpose to my visit."

"And what might that be?" I asked, still not certain who was standing before me.

"Frankly, I've heard you are in big trouble and I've come to help. If what I've heard about GlobalView since my return from the Himalayas is true, you cannot afford not to listen to what I've come to tell you. I've discovered information that will return you and your business to the heights of success you once enjoyed. I've been given knowledge that will lead you to certain market leadership. I've learned lessons that will show you how to have the most loyal, dedicated and inspired employees of any company in your field. This information was given to me by a very learned teacher, who I met high in the mountains. The timeless wisdom he shared with me is not widely known here in the West. Yet it is so potent and so very profound that I am certain it will revolutionize your entire organization and do wonders for your bottom line."

"Go on," I replied, my curiosity piqued.

"The wisdom I've come to share with you is contained within a unique and extremely powerful system, a leadership blueprint of sorts. It's actually foolproof. Follow the system and then just sit back and watch your company return to prime health. Well, actually, it's designed to do far more than that. If you follow the formula with conviction, your business will be much more successful than it ever was. It will improve it in ways you never could have

Julian chuckled but then quickly returned to the point he was making. "You brush your teeth every single morning and wouldn't dream of not doing it. So it's a perfect example of a ritual. If you can integrate the leadership truths from Yogi Raman's system into your routine to the same degree, your success as a visionary leader will be guaranteed. This I promise you."

"Great, I'm feeling excited already. So far you've explained that enlightened and effective leaders all have a vividly imagined future vision. They know precisely where they want to go and concentrate their energies on getting there. You've also taught me that the leadership truths that make up Yogi Raman's timeless success system need to be made into rituals so that I practice them daily, almost unconsciously, in spite of how busy I get. Would it be possible for you to give me the elements of this ancient system now?" I asked, barely containing my curiosity.

Julian looked up to the sky, which had now grown dark and star-filled. He gazed for what seemed like an eternity at one star in particular, squinting his eyes in an effort to see it more clearly. Then he muttered something under his breath. While I couldn't make out all that he said, I did hear, "So there you are, my friend. I've missed you for a while."

Then, realizing that he had drifted off, he quickly caught himself and returned his attention to me, looking mildly embarrassed. "Sorry about that, Peter. When one spends as much time alone as I do, one's social graces tend to diminish. I apologize for my mind wandering off like that. It's just that I spotted something I haven't been able to find all week."

After a moment, he continued. "Yogi Raman taught me that there were a series of specific rituals practiced by visionary leaders, eight to be precise. These eight disciplines represented a distillation of all the leadership wisdom that had been passed down through the ages and practiced by the world's greatest leaders of people. These were not the quick-fix, flavor-of-the-month strategies that are so prevalent in today's businessplace. Instead, they reflected the ageless truths about how to deeply stir men and women into action, how to cultivate tremendous loyalty and respect and how to bring out the very best in the people you lead. Yogi Raman, in all his brilliance, fashioned these eight rituals into the leadership system I've promised to share with you for some time now. You have been patient and sincere in your interest to learn a better way to lead. And so the time has come for me to teach the system to you."

"Would it be fair to assume that the piece of the puzzle you left with me yesterday after your surprise visit to my office has something to do with the first ritual of Yogi Raman's leadership system?"

"Indeed it does, Peter. The First Ritual of Visionary Leaders is Link Paycheck to Purpose. Simply put, this is the ritual of a compelling future focus. As I have already told you, all enlightened leaders have a richly imagined vision of their organization's future. But having a vision is not enough. The vision must excite the minds and touch the hearts of the men and women of your organization. People will go far beyond the call of duty when their leader paints for them a future vision that is compelling and important. *Purpose is the most powerful motivator in the world.*

"Yogi Raman told me that one of the greatest human hungers is the need we all have to make a difference in the lives of others. People have a deep inner need to be a part of something larger than themselves. Whether we are speaking of the CEO or the shipping clerk, every human being needs to feel that he or she is making some sort of contribution. Great leaders appreciate this hunger and constantly communicate to their followers how what they do in their daily work positively affects the world at large. They also fan the flames of excitement within their organizations by continually showing their people that the work they are doing is moving them closer to a compelling cause. To put it simply, these leaders give their followers a reason to get up in the morning."

"Very interesting. Any ideas on how I could apply this to my situation?"

"Earlier you said that low morale is stifling GlobalView's growth."

"True."

"Then remember this, Peter. There's no such thing as an unmotivated person, only an unmotivated employee. You can take any member of your team whom you believe lacks motivation and initiative and scrutinize his or her personal life and guess what you'll see?"

"Dare I guess?"

"You will see that that person has hobbies that he loves. You will see that he has interests that excite him. You will discover that he works late into the night on his stamp collection or spends hours learning new languages or passionately playing musical instruments. Every single person on this planet has the ability to get excited and motivated about something. The leader's primary task is to get his team excited and motivated about the compelling cause that is his vision. Rather than constantly ordering your people to work toward the future goals you have developed, why not give them a reason to do so? And if you find that they are still unmotivated, understand that it is because you still have not given them enough reasons to buy into your picture of the future. Remember what the psychologists have known for many years:

human beings naturally move away from pain and toward pleasure. Visionary leaders find ways to associate pleasure with the daily work of their employees and the ultimate cause they are working toward. *They link paycheck to purpose.*"

Julian continued. "What's your current corporate mission statement?"

"C'mon, I'm tired of hearing about mission statements. I think that whole idea has been done to death, if you don't mind me saying so."

"I agree. But the fact remains that crafting a statement of your organization's future can only serve to refocus the energies of your people on the things that count. So bear with me, please."

"To be the preferred supplier of our customers, to create high-quality products and to grow into a five-billion-dollar company within five years," I stated proudly.

"Do you truly think a mission statement like that will inspire people to give their best to the company? Do you seriously believe you have given your people a reason to get out of bed every morning? Have you really shown them a compelling cause they can work toward? Every company wants to be the customer's preferred supplier. And about the five billion dollars, I'll let you in on a secret. You're probably the only one in the entire company who is excited about that one. It has no *emotional* impact on the average person within the organization, working hard to pay off the mortgage and to put her kids through school."

Julian's words stung me. I knew he wanted to challenge me to explore new pathways of thought. But he was hitting pretty close to home. I had drawn up that mission statement myself. And it meant a lot to me.

"Let's look for ways to reframe your future vision to make it more compelling to those you lead. What business are you in?"

"We make software."

"And what is your primary market?"

"The health-care field. Our software is used primarily by major hospitals and health-care providers to better serve their patients."

"Ah, now we're getting somewhere," Julian replied. "And what exactly does your software allow your customers to do?"

"Well, our bestselling program assists doctors and nurses in the monitoring of critical-care patients. Though it was only developed last year, our industry trade magazine recently reported that that piece of software alone has saved over 100,000 lives."

"Now that's what I mean by a compelling cause," said Julian with great enthusiasm. "And what kind of revenue would GlobalView be generating if you were saving millions of lives?"

"That's really hard to say. There are so many factors that I'd have to consider and —"

"For the purposes of the point I'm trying to make, let's be very flexible with the numbers," Julian interrupted. "Just tell me, is it possible that if the software program you are selling saved millions and millions of lives each year, the revenues of your company could rise to five billion?"

"Yes, it's possible," I admitted.

"Fine then. Imagine your mission statement was amended to read, 'GlobalView is passionately committed to saving the lives of men, women and children by providing our respected customers with cutting-edge, high-value software that allows them to brilliantly serve their patients' needs. Our five-year goal is to save the lives of over five million people and make a significant and lasting impact on the health-care industry."

"Wow," I replied, immediately understanding the power of the lesson Julian was presenting.

"You see, Peter, *the job of every leader is to define reality for his people.* He shows his people a better, brighter, more enlightened way to see the world. He takes the challenges they face and reframes them as opportunities for growth, improvement and success. He does more than show people *how* to do things right — that is the job of the manager. The enlightened leader clarifies the right things to do, which gives his people compelling reasons to do what they do better than they have ever done it. He constantly reaffirms that the purpose everyone is striving toward is a good one and a just one and an honorable one. He understands that the best motivator for innovative and exceptional performance is meaningful work.

"And the truly visionary leader offers his followers hope by showing them that a higher reality exists for them if they keep moving in the direction of the leader's vision. To put it another way, he instills a sense of passion within his people by engaging their hearts and minds through the power of his purpose. Napoleon Hill captured the sentiment when he said, 'Cherish your vision and your dreams as they are the children of your soul; the blueprints of your ultimate achievements,' while Orison Swett Marden wrote, 'There is no medicine like hope, no incentive so great, and no tonic so powerful as expectation for something better tomorrow.' Find a vision you can invest every ounce of yourself within, one that will become your driving force, your raison d'etre, your life's work. The excitement and positive energy that you will generate will spill over into the entire organization."

"That makes so much sense, Julian. If I imagine a truly compelling cause or worthy vision for the future of GlobalView and effectively communicate it to my employees in a way that fulfills their hunger to contribute and make a real difference, they *will* get excited about their work."

"Absolutely. Oh, and don't forget, stop being so focused on *what* you will get when you realize your vision and begin to pay more attention to the *why* of what you are doing. By dedicating your energies to the worthy purpose lying behind what you are doing and taking the focus off the rewards, you will get to your destination far more quickly."

"Why's that?"

"I'll tell you a fable that Yogi Raman shared with me that will answer your question nicely. Once a young student traveled many miles to find a famous spiritual master. When he finally met this man, he told him that his main goal in life was to be the wisest man in the land. This is why he needed the best teacher. Seeing the young boy's enthusiasm, the master agreed to share his knowledge with him and took him under his wing. 'How long will it take before I find enlightenment?' the boy immediately asked. 'At least five years,' replied the master. 'That is too long,' said the boy. 'I cannot wait five years! What if I study twice as hard as the rest of your students?' 'Ten years,' came the response. 'Ten years! Well, then how about if I studied day and night, with every ounce of my mental concentration? Then how long would it take for me to become the wise man that I've always dreamed of becoming?' 'Fifteen years,' replied the master. The boy grew very frustrated. 'How come every time I tell you I will work harder to reach my goal, you tell me it will take longer?' 'The answer is clear,' said the teacher. 'With one eye focused on the reward, there is only one eye left to focus on your purpose.'"

"I won't forget that one, Julian."

"It's full of truth, isn't it? Rather than focusing on what he could give by reaching his ultimate destination, the boy's mind was centered on what he would receive. And therefore, it would take him far longer to get there. What I'm really trying to say, Peter, is that *you need to concentrate on contribution. Giving begins the receiving process*, that's the irony. By rallying around a worthy cause and constantly asking, 'How can we serve?' the rewards flow in degrees you cannot imagine. As they say in the East, 'A little bit of fragrance always clings to the hand that gives you roses.'"

"So true, when one really thinks about it," I admitted.

"Here's a great example. Southwest Airlines has consistently been one of the most successful major airlines. Herb Kelleher, its feisty and innovative leader, could easily have defined the purpose of the company in terms of "being a great airline" or in terms of levels of profit or in terms of customer satisfaction. But he didn't. He had the wisdom to understand that by rallying his people around an emotionally compelling cause, Southwest would become a great airline, make huge profits and generate an army of satisfied customers. So he defined his company's work — and its reality — in a way that truly connected with people."

"How did he do that?"

"He explained that Southwest was a very special airline run by very special people. He showed his team how the low fares the company advertised allowed people who could previously never afford air travel the opportunity to fly on a regular basis. This meant that grandparents could start visiting their grandchildren more frequently and that small-business people could explore markets they never could have before. He showed his people how their work was really about helping others fulfill their dreams and live better lives. He understood that *one of the key tasks of the visionary leader is to engage hearts.*

"And once he did, everything else he hoped for followed. So find a way for you and your managers to show your people their work, directly or indirectly, touches people's lives. Show them that they are needed and important and satisfy their hunger to make a difference. This is what the First Ritual of Visionary Leaders is all about. *Because when you link paycheck to purpose, you connect people to a cause higher than themselves. Your people will start to feel good about what they are doing. And when your people feel good about the work they do, they will begin to feel good about themselves as people. That's when real breakthroughs start to happen.* As Henry Ford once said, 'No one is apathetic except those in pursuit of someone else's objectives.' Give your people a slice of ownership in your vision. They will reward you with the gift of fidelity to your leadership."

"Come to think of it," I interjected, "Recently I heard of a similar example of connecting to a compelling cause. During World War II, the workers who made parachutes for the Allied Forces were less than enthusiastic about their jobs, which could be described as tedious at best. They spent their days doing the same things over and over again and eventually grew weary of their work. Then one day, one of the leaders of their organization sat them all down and reminded them of the value of their work. He told them that it just might save the lives of their own fathers, sons, brothers and compatriots. He reminded them that their work saved lives. By reconnecting them to the big picture, he made productivity go through the roof."

Julian then reached over to pick up a newspaper someone had left on the table next to us, which he thrust in front of me. As I squinted to see the picture on the front page in the dim porch light, Julian remarked, "I read the paper earlier today and came up with an insight I'd like to share with you. What do you see right here on this page?"

"Looks like a photo of the earth, like the ones the space-shuttle astronauts have been taking."

"Right. This afternoon, under the midday sun, I looked at that newspaper photo with my magnifying glass. Guess what I saw?"

"No idea."

"I saw that it was actually made up of nothing more than thousands of tiny black dots. Try it yourself tomorrow morning over a cup of coffee. You'll see that every single picture in the entire paper is nothing more than a collection of ink dots."

"Okay, so what's your point, Julian?"

"My point is that when you ask someone what the subject matter of this photograph is he or she will quickly tell you that it is of the earth. No one will ever tell you he or she sees ten thousand dots clumped together. When viewing the pictures in the newspaper, we have trained ourselves to focus on the big picture, to observe the subject matter from a higher perspective. Yet, too often in business, leaders and managers lose all perspective and spend their days focusing on the little things."

"On the dots," I interjected, grasping the power of Julian's excellent analogy.

"You got it. And in doing so, they miss a world of opportunities, just like anyone focusing on the dots that make up this picture would miss this spectacular view of our world. To be a visionary leader, you must stay focused on the big picture — the compelling cause that lies at the heart of your vision. You must keep your people centered on the communities they are helping and on the lives they are touching. That will provide all the motivation they need."

"But doesn't it take a special kind of person to want to work hard for his or her company because it is doing good work and advancing 'an emotionally compelling cause' to use your words? I'll be honest, all my people care about is getting their paychecks. They couldn't care less about the company or the vision it has."

"That's your fault."

"What do you mean?"

"Stop blaming your people for your leadership failures. Stop blaming the changing economy, increased regulation and competitive pressures. If people haven't bought in to your vision, it's because they haven't bought in to your leadership. If they are not loyal, it's because you have not given them enough reasons to be loyal. If they are not passionate about their work, it's because you have failed to give them something to be passionate about. Assume total responsibility, Peter. Understand that *great leadership precedes great followership.*"

The truth of what Julian had just said rocked me. None of the management seminars I'd attended or consultants I'd worked with had ever offered me this kind of insight. And yet I knew it was right. Something inside me, intuition perhaps, confirmed that this youthful and vibrant-looking man in the robes of a monk was sharing the kind of wisdom that would profoundly affect my leadership and even my life. I knew I lacked a clear vision for the future and that all those around me could sense this failure. I knew my sense of uncertainty about the future was being telegraphed throughout the company by my temper tantrums and lack of confidence. And I knew my people did not respect or trust me. Julian was absolutely right. They had not bought in to my leadership.

"Great followership begins the day your people sense you truly have their best interests in mind," Julian continued. "Only when they know you care about them as people will they go to the wall for you. When you start putting your people before your profits you will have accomplished something even more powerful than engaging their hearts. You will have earned their trust. Never forget that the real secret to being seen as trustworthy is to be worthy of trust."

It was now 10:00 P.M. and Julian and I were the only two people remaining on the golf club's verandah. I thought of suggesting to my friend that we move our conversation over to my home but then decided against it. The night was nothing short of perfect. The sky was strikingly clear and glittered with a thousand stars. A full moon illuminated the area where we sat and lent a mystical feeling to what had already been a most unusual day. Julian was deeply engrossed in our conversation and the leadership wisdom was flowing out of him with eloquence and grace. I would be a fool to do anything else but listen intently to this man who had learned so much during his time high in the Himalayas. I owed at least this to the people in my company.

"Mind if I ask you another basic question, Julian?"

"Not at all. That's why I'm here," he replied.

"How do visionary leaders show their followers that they really do have their best interests in mind?"

"Excellent question, Peter. The first thing to do is to practice the Principle of Alignment."

"Never heard of it."

"The Principle of Alignment holds that when your emotionally compelling cause, what we have simply called your 'vision,' is aligned with the interests of the people under your leadership, you will generate enormous levels of trust, loyalty and commitment. Make sure your future vision is shared by all those you lead. *Too many vision statements hang on office walls rather than live in human hearts.* Give your people, from your top managers to your frontline workers, a genuine sense of ownership in the cause your organization is moving toward. A *shared* vision lies at the heart of every world-class organization."

"And how do I accomplish this?"

"You must show them that by helping you achieve your future goals they will also realize *their* future goals. By integrating what is meaningful to you with what is meaningful to them or, at the very least, by showing them how the attainment of the vision you hold for the company will help them feel fulfilled, they will come to understand that you care about their hopes and dreams. They will come to trust you. And with trust dominating the corporate culture, achievements once viewed as impossible become probable."

Julian added: "There is a second way to gain the respect and loyalty of the men and women you have the privilege to lead. And that is to become a liberator."

I had no idea what he meant, but, not wanting to ask too many silly questions, I simply nodded.

"You have no idea what I'm talking about do you, Peter?" Julian observed.

"No, not really," I admitted, feeling like a school kid might after being caught in a tiny lie.

"Then why did you nod?" he demanded. "I don't mean to come across as being harsh because that's not what I'm about. I'm here this evening as a friend as well as a teacher who will give you the knowledge you need to fix your dying company and repair your leadership. But be honest. Honesty is one of the most important leadership skills. Remember, truth precedes trust. And people can sense sincerity a mile away. Without it, GlobalView will never grow to greatness."

"Okay, I'm sorry. I just didn't want to look foolish."

"Visionary leaders care more about doing what's right than appearing intelligent. Never forget that. Leadership is not about popularity, it's about integrity. It's not about power, it's about purpose. And it's not about title but rather talent. Which brings me squarely back to the point I was trying to make."

"I'm all ears," I offered sincerely.

"Visionary leaders see themselves as liberators rather than limiters of human talent. Their primary priority is to develop their people's full potential. They realize that every leader's task is to transform the workplace into a place of realized genius. The visionary leader understands that his company must, above all else, become a place and opportunity for self-development and personal fulfillment. He has the wisdom to know that in order for his followers to become deeply committed to his vision and offer the true extent of their capacities he is duty-bound to provide them with challenging work. He must offer them a chance to grow as people through their work. You see, Peter, Yogi Raman told me that another of the human hungers is the need for growth and self-actualization. And visionary leaders satisfy this hunger by freeing people's strengths.

"Every single person on this planet has a deeply felt desire to expand and improve as a person. When you, as a leader, dedicate yourself to liberating rather than stifling the talents of the people under your leadership, you will reap quantum results in terms of loyalty, productivity, creativity and devotion to your compelling cause. The bottom line is simply this: *people who feel superb about themselves generate superb results.* This leadership truth has stood the test of time. Never neglect it.

"The sad fact is that most people have no idea how much talent and potential slumbers within them. William James, the founder of modern psychology, once said, 'Most people live — whether physically, intellectually or morally — in a very restricted circle of their potential being. We all have reservoirs of life to draw upon, of which we do not dream.' And he was right. If the average person caught even a glimpse of how powerful he or she truly is, that individual would be astonished. And yet most people have never taken the time to look within themselves to discover who they really are."

"Did the sages teach you that principle?"

"Yes, they did. As a matter of fact, Yogi Raman loved telling me a story on that very point. According to Indian mythology, all people on earth were once gods. However, they began to abuse their power so the supreme god, Brahma, decided he would take this gift away from them and hide the godhead in a place where they would never find it. One advisor suggested it be buried deep within the ground, but Brahma didn't like that idea. 'Mankind will one day dig deep enough to find it,' he said. Another advisor suggested it be hidden in the deepest part of the ocean. 'No,' said Brahma, 'one day mankind will dive deep enough to discover it.' Yet another advisor suggested the godhead be placed on the highest peak of the highest mountain, but Brahma replied, 'No, mankind will eventually find a way to climb to the top and take it.' After silently thinking about it, the supreme god finally found the ideal resting place for that greatest of all gifts. 'Here's the answer: Let's hide it within man himself. He will never think to look there.' "

"Great story," I offered sincerely.

"What I'm really trying to tell you, Peter, is that all people have more energy and ability within them than they could ever imagine. Your job, as a leader, is to uncover this truth for the benefit of your people."

"I hear what you are saying, Julian. But do you really believe that *everyone* has the potential for genius within them?"

"Genius is all about having an exceptional natural ability. We all have our special gifts and capacities. The problem is that most leaders have never offered their people opportunities to test and liberate those gifts. Rather than showing them what success looks like and then letting them use their creativity and resourcefulness to get there, the vast majority of leaders micromanage and dictate the path to be followed at every step of the way. They treat their team members as children, as if they are absolutely incapable of independent thought. Over time, this type of leadership stifles imagination, energy and spirit. Then the leaders cry about a lack of innovation, productivity and performance. 'Leaders should lead as far as they can and then vanish,' wrote H. G. Wells. 'Their ashes should not choke the fire they have lit.'

"So allow your people to flourish as they work toward your shared vision. Show them the truth about their talents and offer them blinding glimpses of a new world of opportunity. Challenge them and allow them to grow. Let them try new things and learn new skills. Let them fail from time to time, since failure is nothing more than learning how to win — free market research if you will. *Failure is the highway to success.* Understand that the visionary leader has the wisdom to push his people up rather than keep them down. He understands that when his people succeed, he succeeds. He understands exactly what Bernard Gimbel meant when he stated, 'Two things are bad for the heart — running uphill and running down people.' "

Julian's face was now fully animated and his hands were gesturing in his passion for what he was saying. "Yogi Raman put it far more eloquently than I ever could," Julian continued. "Late one night, high in the mountains under a magnificent sky he used a phrase that will always stay with me. It speaks volumes about the essence of visionary leadership."

"What was the phrase?" I asked impatiently.

"He told me that *'The ultimate task of the visionary leader is to dignify and honor the lives of those he leads by allowing them to manifest their highest potential through the work they do.'* "

"Powerful statement," I said softly, looking up at the sky in an effort to let the words soak in.

"And it's true. 'In dreams begin responsibilities,' proclaimed the poet Yeats. The visionary leader owes his people the responsibility of helping them develop and flourish. He understands that *the greatest privilege of leadership is the chance to elevate lives.* You need to keep uncovering the truth about their potential so they can see what they really are and what they truly can achieve. The great psychologist Abraham Maslow said that 'the unhappiness, unease and unrest in the world today are caused by people living far below their capacity' and I know he was right."

"Okay, here's another question. If the visionary leader's primary duty is to bring out the best in his people and bottom-line concerns are not important, how does he measure success?"

"I didn't say that the visionary leader disregards the bottom line, Peter. Of course he understands that for his company to grow, profits must flow. Productivity issues, customer satisfaction and quality are all essential issues that occupy his attention. But first and foremost are the development and enrichment of his people. He actually sees his people as bundles of human potential just waiting to be unleashed for a worthy purpose. And he knows that when people work and live at their highest levels, the profits are certain to come. So to answer your question, the visionary leader measures his success through how many lives he touches and how many people he transforms. He measures his success, not by the extent of his power, but by the number of people he empowers. Makes sense?"

"It does, Julian. It really does. Okay, what comes next?"

"Then once you and your managers have begun to liberate the highest potential of your people, keep clarifying and communicating your great vision for the future. Productivity and passion are the inevitable by-product of men and women working toward an emotionally compelling cause. Inspire them to invest their energies and spirits in it. Allow them to feel it's theirs and understand the implications of its achievement. Nothing focuses the mind better than a future ideal that moves the heart. Abe Lincoln knew this, Gandhi knew this, Mandela knew this, and so did Mother Teresa."

"I'll be totally honest. I still don't have a clear future vision of what you call 'an emotionally compelling cause' that I can get my team to rally around. I really liked your earlier example about saving the lives of five million people. I got excited about that idea and I'm sure my people could as well. I guess that's a great starting point. Do you have any advice about how a leader can actually develop his or her vision for the future?"

"I don't mean to be trite, Peter, but it does take a lot of work.

You need to spend days and weeks reflecting on what things are most meaningful to you and where GlobalView can make the greatest contribution and impact. Take the time to be silent and begin to cultivate the power of your imagination. Envision what you want this organization to look like five, ten and fifteen years from now. Awareness precedes change, so become aware of all the possibilities the future presents.

"Another tactic you can use to define your future vision is to analyze what keeps you up at night. What things are disturbing you and your customers. Go beyond simply satisfying their needs. Every good company does that. Strive to remove the *frustrations* from their lives. That's the real secret to having a loyal core of satisfied customers. Begin to anticipate what things bother them and define your future vision around these. And then here's the fundamental thing you need to do: once you have a clear focus for the future, constantly check it against the present state of operations. If your vision is an inspiring one, you will notice there is a gap. From this gap between where you now are and where you are going will emerge your strategy for change. Then exert your leadership influence to ensure that your blueprint for the future soon becomes the company's reality. Remember, 90 percent of success lies in the implementation and execution. *One of the hallmarks of visionary leadership lies in the translation of positive intentions into tangible results.*"

"So visionary leaders are people of action. They constantly push themselves to find better and faster ways to merge the present with the future and realize their vision. Is that accurate?"

"Yes, it is. They understand the ancient Law of Diminishing Intent and make sure it doesn't apply to them."

"I've never heard of that one."

"The Law of Diminishing Intent says that the longer you wait to implement a new idea or strategy, the less enthusiasm you will have for it. I think anyone who has worked in the corporate world knows the feeling of rushing out of a motivational seminar full of great ideas that will change every aspect of his or her life. But then the demands of the day compete for our attention and all our good intentions and personal promises for change get pushed to the wayside. And the longer we put them off, the lower the probability we will ever fulfill them. So the lesson is to act daily on your strategy for change before it dies a quick death, burying your future vision with it. As the German philosopher Johann von Goethe said many years ago, 'Whatever you can do and dream you can do, begin it. Boldness has genius, power and magic.' "

"So simple and yet so profound, Julian," I responded, trying to fully absorb these words of wisdom.

In the few hours I'd been with Julian this evening, I'd learned more about the craft of leadership than I had in all my previous years in business. Much of it really was common sense, but then, as Voltaire observed, "Common sense is anything but common." I guess I'd just never taken the time to think deeply about the elements of leadership and how I could implement them in our company. My days were filled with so many seemingly immediate brush fires to tend to that I was neglecting the fundamentals of effective leadership.

Ironically, due to this neglect, things were going from bad to worse. It made me think about the story of the lighthouse-keeper that my grandfather used to tell me. The lighthouse-keeper had only a limited amount of oil to keep his beacon lit so that passing ships could avoid the rocky shore. One night, the elderly man who lived close by needed to borrow some oil to light his home, so the lighthouse-keeper gave him some. Another night, a traveler begged for some oil to light his lamp so he could continue his journey. The lighthouse-keeper also complied with this request and gave him the oil he needed. The next night, the lighthouse-keeper was awakened by a mother banging on his door. She prayed for some oil so that she could illuminate her home and feed her family. Again he agreed. Soon all his oil was gone and his beacon went out. Many ships ran aground and many lives were lost because the lighthouse-keeper forgot to focus on his priority. He neglected his primary duty and paid a high price.

I realized I was heading down the same path as the lighthouse-keeper. I was not focusing on the timeless principles of enlightened, effective and visionary leadership that Julian was sharing with me. Unless I simplified my leadership and stopped putting second things first, I sensed that I too would face disaster and be required to pay a particularly high price.

For the first time all night, Julian appeared weary. Many hours had passed since we had met on the verandah and Julian had startled me with his miraculous hole in one. Though he had clearly discovered many of the secrets of personal renewal along with the leadership truths he shared with me, he was still human after all and was entitled to be tired.

"Julian. I am so grateful to you for what you are doing. God knows, I need the coaching. You have spent the entire evening passionately teaching me some very powerful lessons I know will lead to immediate improvements in my organization, once I have the courage to implement them. I could listen to you all night. You always were a great speaker and dynamic conversationalist. But I want to be fair to you. Why don't we call it a night and meet first thing tomorrow morning in my office. I've kept the whole morning free in anticipation of us spending more time together. Let me drive you home now."

"Thanks for the offer, Peter. I must admit that I'm beginning to feel a little sleepy. I know I look like a young man, but you know exactly how old I am. Though I feel more alive and vital now than I did when I was twenty, I still require a few hours of shut-eye to recharge the body and refresh the mind. If you don't mind, I think I'll walk back to where I'm staying. It's not too far from here anyway."

"But we're in the middle of the country, Julian. There's nothing but forest and farmland for miles," I offered, with real concern.

"Don't worry about me," Julian replied, clearly intending to keep his resting place a well-guarded secret. "I'll be just fine."

"So I'll see you tomorrow morning?"

"Actually I'm busy tomorrow morning. And for the next few days, I have other matters I must attend to."

"You're not looking for a new Ferrari?" I joked, fully aware of the reply I would elicit.

"No, Peter. My Ferrari days are over. I've become a simple man bearing the simple truths that our world needs to hear. I promised Yogi Raman and the other sages I would spend the rest of my life sharing their leadership wisdom with those who need to hear it. And that's exactly what I intend to do. How about if we meet next Friday? That will give you some time to contemplate what I've shared with you and put some of the philosophy into practice."

"Sure, Julian. If you want to meet next Friday, next Friday it will be. Same time, same place?"

"Actually, I'd like to meet you at a different location. Let's meet performance will eventually come because your people will keep getting better and better."

"Kind of like our home team here," I said pointing to the players who had just run down the length of the court on a fast break and scored another two points. "I remember coming to see them when the franchise was brand new. Man, they were pathetic. And yet that wasn't really so long ago."

"And many of those same players have become superstars. The coach praised progress. He found a reason to reward them. And now look at these guys. They are unbelievable," Julian said, jumping to his feet again. His fists were now pumping into the air and he was yelling words of encouragement to the players, all of whom he knew by name. I never realized Julian was such a big ball fan. His enthusiasm was contagious.

"Julian, I've got more questions for you."

"Fire away," he said, once again returning to his seat amid the stares of those who had the misfortune to be seated near us.

"I'm not really sure I know what to say when I praise someone. I mean, I've never really done it before. Sure I can say a few quick words like 'nice job' or 'keep it up,' but do you have any other suggestions on effective praising?"

"Praising is a skill that requires study and practice. Every leader needs to get good at it. To get you started, here are a few of the basic praise principles: praise must be specific, it must be immediate, it must be done in public and it must be sincere. Also, personalize your praise by using the person's first name when making the positive comment. The most beautiful sound in the world to a person is the sound of his or her own name. Oh, and don't fall into the trap that too many managers fall into when they praise."

"Which is?"

"They overpraise. While praise is important, giving it with reckless abandon devalues it, just like printing too much money cheapens the currency."

"Any other specific ideas on motivating my team?"

"Sure. I'll give you some of the best and most cost-effective ones. Posting a personal thank-you note on the employee's door, paying his parking expenses for a month, an annual subscription to the magazine of his choice are simple but proven ways to reward people for excellent performance. Letting an employee attend a meeting for his manager, sending birthday cards and breaking bread with employees also help to keep them motivated and show you care. I recently read about one manager who adopted the low-cost but highly effective strategy of filling a large chest full of motivational books, tapes and videos from respected personal development authors. She called this her 'treasure chest.' When any of her team members deserved to be rewarded, she would walk them over to the chest, in full public view, and encourage them to select something they'd enjoy. I love this idea because it not only rewards good behavior, it allows your people to grow and develop through their exposure to the positive books, tapes and videos, making them even better performers.

"Remember, Peter, visionary leaders are liberators, not limiters. They know they are duty-bound to help people unlock the best that lies within them and to help them develop a sense of stewardship over their professional and personal lives. They constantly expose their employees to ideas and information that will help them actualize their natural talents and become more independent as thinkers and as people. As the great sage Confucius observed, *'Give a man a fish and you feed him for a day. Teach a man to fish and you feed him for a lifetime.'* Like I told you at the clubhouse that night, leadership is all about freeing people's strengths. When you really get down to it, the actual corporation you call GlobalView isn't much more than a seal and a few pieces of paper spewed out from some corporate lawyer's computer. The true value lies in your people and their potential to help you manifest your grand vision for the future."

"Powerful thoughts. You know now that I think about it, some of our competitors have some pretty good techniques to energize their employees as well."

"Really?"

"I guess I just didn't understand the power of rewarding and recognition, so I didn't pay much attention to them."

"When the student is ready the teacher appears," said Julian with a smile as the game drew to a close.

"One of GlobalView's competitors is constantly doing fun things to challenge and stimulate its team. Its sales team always begins meetings by 'celebrating heroes,' going around the table recognizing the salespeople for meeting their goals or for excellence in customer care. Another company has dubbed one office wall 'the victory wall,' placing motivational quotes, testimonial letters and strategic goals on it for all to see as they pass by. I've even heard about one top Xerox manager who took a ski cap embroidered with the name of a five-star ski resort to every meeting. This 'symbol of victory' served as a powerful reminder of where the team would be vacationing if it met its sales targets."

"Those are fabulous ideas I think you should seriously consider bringing into your organization. And never forget the importance of cultural traditions."

"Run that one by me again," I requested.

"In the Himalayas, the sages had developed a whole series of cultural traditions to keep them unified. Every evening, no matter how busy they were with their philosophical readings or teachings, they would come together to share a simple but delicious meal around a long wooden table. It was really an unbelievable sight to watch these beautifully adorned monks laughing and singing as they ate, savoring the gifts of one another's company and enriching their sense of community. These basketball players do the same thing with their Friday-night pizza parties or their semi-annual family picnics. These are traditions that serve to bring people closer. They encourage teammates to care about one another. They build richer relationships and help people to see themselves as a part of a shared destiny."

"So traditions should become part of our corporate culture?"

"Definitely. Let people get to know one another and let their hair down from time to time. Have family picnics or biweekly submarine-sandwich lunches. Shake the cobwebs out of those huge headquarters you have and get people talking and laughing again. One company I know of even has Crazy Days. Believe me, people not only have a great time, productivity soars. As one wise leader once said, 'Brains, like hearts, go where they are appreciated.' "

"Explain this Crazy Days tradition to me. I've never heard of it."

"In this particular company, a day is designated every quarter as a Crazy Day. It's nothing more than a day designed to let people blow off steam and reduce stress; it boosts morale. For example, one quarter, they designated it as You're Not the Boss Day. The CEO had to make coffee, answer the phones and work in the warehouse while some of his employees got to work out of the boss's office and have some fun. This simple idea broke down many of the artificial barriers between management and nonmanagement people and enhanced team spirit. Another quarter, the crazy day was called Corporate Circus Day. Clowns, magicians and jesters were hired to perform throughout the company's offices, much to the delight of all the employees. Even those passing by the lobby were invited to take part in the spectacle, providing great word-of-mouth promotion about this innovative and people-centered organization. One of the most successful crazy days was Back to the Future Day."

"Sounds intriguing."

"All the employees got together to celebrate their past successes. Personal success stories were posted on the walls of the conference hall that had been rented for the occasion, for everyone to see. Then they all focused on their future goals and brainstormed about the best ways to achieve them.

"The point I'm trying to make with all these examples is that visionary leaders understand that employees who feel they are valued members of an exciting team will go the extra mile to give their best. If you practice Ritual 3 by rewarding routinely and recognizing relentlessly, they will invest their spirits in your organization. And they will begin to see themselves as a part of the larger whole, as an integral part of something special and as an important member of the GlobalView team. That's when your company will become unstoppable. Perhaps Yogi Raman said it best the time he observed that 'when spider webs unite they can tie up a lion.'"

As the crowd filtered out of the stadium, a strange silence filled the air. We had won the game and people were clearly pleased.

But something even more pressing had attracted everyone's attention. Up in the sky, one star had begun to twinkle brightly, illuminating the darkness with an almost magical hue. Though it was almost 11:00 P.M., it appeared as if a rich coat of daylight was waiting to burst through the darkness and envelope the night sky.

I had never seen a phenomenon such as this. Soon the entire crowd was standing still, staring quietly into the sky.

"I can't believe what I'm seeing, Julian," I said, my gaze fixed on the bright star that appeared to be the center of everyone's attention.

"I can," he replied with a knowing smile.

"Does this have something to do with the star you were talking to the other night and that telescope you are carrying?" I asked intently.

"Absolutely. And the time will soon come when I can explain exactly what's going on. When I was in the Himalayas, the sages predicted that this astronomical event would take place. Even I'm surprised at how accurate they were."

Within minutes, the darkness had returned and the glittering star had quietly slipped off into the night. The sight I had just witnessed was astonishing. Though I didn't know anything about astronomy and such natural occurrences, the magnificence of the spectacle was almost overwhelming.

"That was incredible, Julian!"

"The laws of nature are the most powerful laws in the universe," he replied. "They lead you to the truth, Peter. The quality of our lives as leaders is better off by the degree to which we learn from them. Visionary leaders have full knowledge of these laws and align their efforts with them."

"What do you mean?"

"They have the leadership wisdom to understand that 'as you sow, so shall you reap.' They know that the growth of a business follows the same cyclical process as the change of seasons. They are aware that, as in nature, adversity is always followed by opportunity, just as the darkness of the night is always followed by the brightness of the day."

"I've never thought that the laws of nature applied to the business world."

"They sure do and the leader who recognizes this timeless fact will have an enormous advantage over his or her competition. That's why our next meeting will be in more natural surroundings."

"Where exactly?"

"I'd like us to meet next Sunday in the woods behind Bear Lake."

"You mean the place where all those hunters go?"

"Precisely. Just go to the entrance of the forest. From there, you will see a series of markers that will lead you to the spot where I will continue to share the sages' leadership wisdom with you. I promise that you will not be disappointed."

"What time?"

"At dawn. It's a very special time of the day."

"You're kidding, right?"

"I'm absolutely serious. The dawn is the best part of the day. And I think it's about time you experienced the tranquility it brings. Now I've got to run."

"You're always dashing off, Julian. What's the hurry?"

"I've got to find that star," was the only reply I received as he disappeared into the crowd.

On my way home, my thoughts turned to the wealth of knowledge I had been blessed with on this wonderful evening. I thought about the importance of "rewarding routinely and recognizing relentlessly." I reflected on Julian's point that "praise is free" and how most people go to bed hungry every night, hungry for a little sincere appreciation and respect. I remembered all the men and women of GlobalView who dutifully came into work every morning and spent their days without a word of thanks for the energy they expended. There were the managers and the programmers and the delivery staff who I had never even shown the courtesy of a sincere "good morning, how are you?" These people were not the root cause of our company's troubles — I was. As Julian had said earlier, great leadership precedes great followership. And I had been far less than the great leader they deserved.

I then contemplated the many creative ways my managers and I could start energizing our people and getting them focused on success. Just thinking about the possibilities and the positive results that would come through their application got me excited. We could set up treasure chests full of motivational books and tapes throughout the headquarters to reward good behavior immediately. We could have submarine-sandwich parties from time to time and set up other traditions so that our people could blow off steam and build stronger bonds. You're Not The Boss Day might be a great way to get the word out that I'm not the same old leader I once was. My mind began to fill with new ideas.

How about leaving nonmanagers in charge while my management team and I headed off for the annual two-day retreat I had decided to organize this year? Why not name boardrooms after top employees? Why not reward a worker who comes up with a new revenue-generating idea with a percentage of the profits it generates or at the very least with time off? Perhaps the ten best employees of every division could dine with me and the rest of our top executives every quarter? And I would certainly be sending out hundreds of thank-you notes over the coming months. A little praise could go a long way, I realized.

Upon entering the lobby of our luxury high rise, I reached into the pocket of the light coat I was wearing for my keys when I felt a foreign object. As I moved into the hallway, a smile came to my face. The light revealed that the object was the next piece of the jigsaw puzzle. Julian must have slipped it in while I was watching the game.

This time the inscription read simply, *Ritual 4: Surrender to Change.*

Chapter 7 Knowledge Summary • Julian's Wisdom in a Nutshell

The Ritual

Reward Routinely, Recognize Relentlessly™

The Essence

The Ritual of Team Unity

The Wisdom

- Great leaders are great teachers and great coaches
- Reward and recognize employees regularly. Give genuine appreciation. You always get more of what you reward.
- Praise is free

The Practices

- Hunt for good behavior
- The 'Treasure Chest' and 'Victory Wall'
- Symbols of Victory and team traditions

Quotable Quote

Visionary leaders understand that employees who feel they are valued members of an exciting team will go the extra mile and give their best. If you practice ritual 2 by rewarding routinely and recognizing relentlessly, they will invest their spirits in your organization. They will begin to see themselves as part of a larger whole. That is when your company will become unstoppable.

The Monk Who Sold His Ferrari

RITUAL 4

❦

Surrender to Change

The Ritual of Adaptability and Change Management

Watch and see the courses of the stars as if you ran with them, and continually dwell in mind upon the changes of the elements into one another; for these imaginations wash away the foulness of life on the ground.

Marcus Aurelius

I could not believe I had agreed to meet Julian at this ungodly hour. Not surprisingly, there was no one in sight as I marched up to the entrance to the forest, carrying a Thermos full of coffee and a bag full of pastries, which I hoped Julian might share with me. A remarkable stillness pervaded the scene as I proceeded into the woods. The first rays of daylight peeped through the dense arrangement of trees, guiding me deeper into this natural oasis of calm.

As I walked, the fragrance of pine and cedar tickled my nose, bringing back so many warm memories from my childhood when my father and I would venture into the timberland on long hikes. Sometimes we would even bring our old canoe and go for long paddles on sun-soaked lakes. Those were some of the best times of my life. I don't know how I got so far away from nature. Right then and there, I resolved to renew the connection. I knew getting back to nature and its inherent peacefulness would allow me to be a better leader and a deeper thinker. As William Wordsworth observed, "When from our better selves we have too long been parted by the hurrying world, sick of its business, of its pleasures tired, how gracious, how benign is solitude." Such wonderful words.

Just then, I noticed what appeared to be a map stuck to the trunk of a large pine tree with a wooden nail. Julian had said there would be markings for me to follow to get to where he would be; this was certainly one of them. I took a moment to study the prescribed route and then ventured farther into the forest. The instructions that had been scribbled onto the map indicated I was to travel north for half a mile. Once there, I would see a small stream that I was to cross and then follow for another mile. This would lead me to what the scribbling said was the Final Resting Place. I had no idea what that meant and didn't wish to worry myself by analyzing it.

I pushed on, growing tired and out of breath after twenty minutes of walking. Sweat dripped from my forehead and onto the soft floor of the forest while my heart beat wildly out of control. But if there was one quality I had always had, it was the fighting spirit. I never gave up, no matter what obstacles I encountered. My father used to tell me there were four elements of one's character that if cultivated, guaranteed success: The first element was discipline, the second, concentration, the third element was patience and the fourth one, persistence. I always took those words seriously. And so I trudged on.

Suddenly I heard a noise coming from a distant area. It was

soft at first but then grew more noticeable. It sounded like an animal running through the bushes, breaking the small twigs that littered the ground as it moved. Perhaps it was a raccoon or a fox or maybe even a small deer. But then, to my utter surprise, I saw that it was a human figure, swiftly moving among the trees, clutching what appeared to be a long wooden stake! I could not tell if it was a man or a woman and I was not about to call out and ask. I darted in the opposite direction, genuinely afraid for my safety. After all, there was no help available for miles and the sight of that sharp wooden stake was less than comforting.

My heart raced even more fiercely and the sweat began to flow like a torrent as I fought my way through the brush, now running as fast as my legs could travel. My Thermos full of coffee and the fresh pastries had been left behind as I cut my way deeper and deeper into the forest. Finally, after running for a little more than half an hour, I realized the figure was nowhere in sight. I immediately collapsed and lay on the ground, surrounded by bright flowers and small evergreens. Looking up through the trees, I caught glimpses of the blue sky. It was a cloudless summer's day. Perfect really. Too bad I didn't have the energy to move.

My thoughts then turned to Julian. Surely that wasn't him back there with the stake. Why would he have wanted to scare me? And if it was Julian, at least he would have had the courtesy to reveal himself to me. I then grew angry. Here I was, in the middle of a forest notorious for bears, cougars and wolves and Julian was nowhere in sight. He had said there would be markers that would lead me to him, but I hadn't seen them. To make matters worse, a deranged lunatic with a wooden dagger was hunting for me, and I had no idea how to get back to my four-wheel drive. As a matter of fact, I was totally lost.

'Okay. I need to pull myself together,' I thought to myself. 'I'm the CEO of a two-billion-dollar company. I have a wonderful wife and two great children whom I love deeply and who need me. I'm going to find my way out of this.'

As I stood up, I heard the something that offered me the hope I was searching for. It was the sound of a stream, flowing along an area of the forest that was much less densely vegetated. I realized this must have been the stream that appeared on the map Julian had left for me. If I crossed the stream, as his instructions had indicated, and followed it for one mile, I would find the Final Resting Place. But which direction was I to travel the one mile in?

I made a guess and headed down the stream. As I progressed, a sense of calmness began to return. Maybe it was the effect of the natural surroundings, the likes of which I had not seen in years. Or perhaps it was because this was the first occasion in a long time that I had taken the time to be by myself.

Eventually, the stream meandered past a particularly rocky area and then along the banks of a large meadow. As I climbed up into this clearing, I saw something very startling. In the center of the meadow stood a small hut made entirely of what appeared to be roses. Surrounding the hut was a vegetable garden and hundreds of exotic flowers. Butterflies flitted through the air, which was laden with a wonderful scent. The whole sight was dazzling. I knew I had found Julian.

"Hello," I called out. "Are you in there, Julian?"

The door of the hut immediately swung open and out came my old friend, beaming. "What took you so long?" he asked. "I've been expecting you for quite a while."

"You wouldn't believe it if I told you. I came here at the crack of dawn, just as you asked. I found your map, read your instructions and started into the woods. I was having a brilliant time until, all of a sudden, some madman started chasing me with a huge wooden stake. I panicked and started to run until I couldn't run any farther. Luckily I lost him and found that stream. It led me right to you. I think I need a drink to calm down. You wouldn't have any of that expensive Scotch you used to drink, would you?"

"My Scotch days are long gone. And as for the madman, don't worry. I know for certain that he wasn't chasing you," Julian said with a surprising degree of certainty.

"How do you know that?"

"Because it was me. I was running through the woods to get this new stake back to this hut before you arrived. You see, this is my home and I'm planning to do some renovations. I needed the stake to hold up 'the new wing'," he laughed.

"That was you?" I exclaimed. "Julian, I thought I was going to die. Why in God's name didn't you let me know? I could have had a heart attack!"

Julian put his arm around my shoulder in an effort to comfort me. "I almost did. But then a thought came to me. The reason I invited you here today, into this miraculous forest hideaway where I live, is to share the power of Ritual 4 with you. Ritual 4, as you know from my little gift to you the other night, requires you to Surrender to Change.

"I thought that if you were exposed to a little adventure and discomfort, you might have an even better appreciation of the lessons I planned to share. I sincerely apologize if I frightened you. But I knew you'd be okay. As a matter of fact, I was watching out for your safety at every step of the way. Now, please come into my home and let's get started. We have an important day of learning ahead of us."

Calming down, I asked, "But what do you mean by Surrender to Change? And how would getting me to feel uncomfortable be of any benefit?"

"Change is the most dominant force in the business world today, as I'm sure you know. Technology is changing, society is changing, the political landscape is changing, even the way people work is changing. Did you know that in the early 1900s, 85 percent of the workers in our part of the world were in agriculture? Now this field involves less than 3 percent of the work force. And it was recently reported that more information has been produced in the past thirty years than in the entire 5,000-year period before it!"

"I'm not surprised. Change is driving us crazy at GlobalView. By the time one of our products hits the market it's actually obsolete since we are already testing something even more advanced. People are demanding new methods of doing their work, we are facing more regulation than ever before, our customers' expectations have totally changed and our competition is now truly global. It seems that by the time we finally come to grips with one new development, ten more come along."

"Precisely. That's why I asked you to come here, to the Final Resting Place as I jokingly call my little home, to learn about Ritual 4, the ritual of adaptability and change management. You see, every visionary leader goes beyond struggling with change. He or she has the wisdom to realize that if one truly wants to master change, one must *surrender* to it."

"And why would scaring the living daylights out of me help me do this?" I asked, puzzled by the charade Julian had put me through.

"Because the only way to manage change is to become good at managing the unexpected. In order to thrive in the new economy, where intellectual capital is far more valuable than material

capital, a leader must master the art of being resilient and react-
ing to unforeseen challenges with grace, agility and speed. Sorry
to say, my friend, but you failed on all counts."

"I don't follow you."

"Well, my little experiment back there was designed to shake
you up and force you to move out of that region of security I've
noticed you live your whole life within. From what I gather, you are
a creature of routine and never try anything new. You barricade
yourself into that massive office of yours and do the same things
day in and day out. When something new comes along, a new skill
to learn or a new challenge to tackle, you try to delegate it to
someone else. At best, you rush to apply the same solutions that
have worked in the past to every one of the new problems you
encounter. And that's one of the reasons why your company is on
the decline rather than seizing the incredible opportunities this
new age of business offers.

*"Doing the same things every day will not deliver new results.
To change the results you are getting, you must change the things
you are doing.* You must transform the way you are leading. Never
forget what Einstein said, 'The significant problems we face cannot
be solved at the same level of thinking we were at when we created
them.' You must think new, higher, bolder thoughts to manage the
change that is bombarding your organization in these topsy-turvy
times. You need to become good at tolerating ambiguity and uncertainty. You must embrace the change."

"Is that what you mean by surrendering to change?"

"Yes. For most leaders, there are only two responses to the
stress that change inevitably brings: fight or flight. You chose the
latter when faced with an unexpected encounter in the woods back
there. But there is a third option to managing change and this is

the practice favored by visionary leaders. They surrender to change and, in doing so, use it to their advantage."

"But isn't that a contradiction? If you surrender or submit to change, doesn't that make you the loser?"

"That is the way we think in the West. In the East, however, the sages and Zen masters have adopted a strikingly different mind-set, one that has proven its effectiveness over the centuries."

"And what might that be?"

"They believe that to conquer, one first must yield. Rather than going against the change, one must go with it. As the ancient philosopher Lao-Tzu said, 'Softness triumphs over hardness. What is more malleable is always superior over that which is immovable. This is the principle of controlling things by going along with them, of mastery through adaption.' Rigidly adhering to tradition and outdated ways of doing things will drive a stake right through the heart of your company. Ralph Waldo Emerson said that a foolish consistency is the hobgoblin of little minds. And he was dead right. Be more flexible, more open and more accepting. Begin to accommodate and align yourself with change. Go with the flow. Be like water," offered Julian. "C'mon. Let's go for a walk."

"Be like water? That's a new one," I said, as we headed down to the stream.

"The nature of water is to flow," Julian observed as he dipped his youthful hand into the bubbling brook. "It goes with the current. It does not resist. It does not hesitate before it yields. But it is also one of the most powerful forces on the earth. Study water and manage the changing currents of modern business like water manages the currents of nature. Rather than viewing change as an adversary, welcome it as a friend. *And then surrender to it.* That's what adaptability is all about."

"Is adaptability that important?"

"Adaptability is one of the most essential leadership skills of our new information-driven world. The leader who can adapt to change and use it to his or her advantage will have a huge competitive edge. But adaptability is more than just going with the change rather than against it. Adaptability is all about recovering from the anxiety and adversity that change initially brings and then having the flexibility to move ahead vigorously. It's about seeing failure as nothing more than market research. It's about understanding that you perfect your abilities by suffering setbacks and that change can allow you and GlobalView to emerge stronger than ever before. It's about persisting until you get to the place where you have determined you must go. Remember, you can't learn to sail without tipping the boat over a few times and you can't learn to play the piano without hitting a few wrong notes. Success is a numbers game and setbacks are a part of it. As the Buddhist saying goes, 'The arrow that hits the bull's eye is the result of one hundred misses.' "

"I've always wondered why I've been so resistant to change. Maybe it's in my genes," I joked.

"Actually that's the perfect explanation," Julian replied in a serious tone. "Every human being is genetically programmed to resist change and maintain a state of equilibrium. The condition, known as *homeostasis*, evolved naturally over time as a means by which our ancestors could survive constantly changing conditions. When an environmental change occurs in our own lives, our internal mechanisms jump into play to regulate the new influence and return the body to what biologists call a *steady state*. Essentially, the condition of equilibrium we call homeostasis developed from our need for stability and security. The problem is that the mechanism works to keep things as they are even when more favorable possibilities exist. It doesn't distinguish between change that would make life better and change that would make things worse. It simply resists all change."

"That's fascinating, Julian. You mean to tell me that every single one of us has been genetically designed to resist change?"

"Yes, and that's why people have such a hard time breaking out of their regions of security. They find it hard to adopt new habits, learn a new skill or cultivate a new attitude. The good news is that homeostats can be reset and change can be embraced. The bad news is that the resetting process always brings stress, pain and a certain amount of fear with it. Your job, as a visionary leader, is to lessen the anxiety by continually reminding your people of why the change is necessary and connecting them to the many benefits that will result from it. Tell them that the change will bring them that much closer to the compelling cause you are all striving toward. Show them how the change will ultimately improve their lives and allow them to be more effective. Make them aware of how the change will help them to serve others and make a deeper contribution. What I'm really saying is help them to master change by giving them the knowledge to change."

"And how do I go about doing that?"

"That brings me to another of the timeless laws of nature, one that is most prevalent in this lush forest I have the privilege to live in — the Law of Environment. A seed grows into a plant only when the soil, moisture and temperature are favorable. In other words the environment must be ideal. Similarly, to manage change effectively, you, as a visionary leader, must provide the ideal culture in which people can respond positively to change and grow in the process."

"And what kind of culture would that be?" I asked with great interest.

"You must create a learning culture. You must champion intellectual development. You must foster a workplace that rewards constant learning and skills improvement. You need to let people know that the best way to combat the fear and strain that change invokes is to become knowledgeable about it. *The best antidote for fear is knowledge.* Don't get lazy about learning. The more prepared and informed your people are, the easier it will be for them to accept and thrive on the change. If you really want to succeed in manifesting your vision for the future into reality, help your people become lifelong learners. To stay competitive in this new era, you must let everyone know they need to be continually learning. Create a corporate culture that inspires them to embrace new ideas and information. And share all the information you have. Remember, Peter, in this day and age, *he or she who learns most wins.*"

As Julian climbed back up the bank of the stream and made his way through the lush meadow, he continued to share the leadership wisdom he had acquired about managing change.

"You see, there is joy in change. Without change, there can be no growth. Without change, there can be no improvement. Without change, there would be no progress. Look at this meadow and the forest you came through. It is in a continuous state of change. The leaves fall off the trees and later reappear. The birds hatch as chicks and evolve into adulthood. The seasons change from winter into spring. Even these butterflies are nothing more than caterpillars who learned to change. Understand that change is the way of the world. Change is essential to our evolution as a civilization. It is necessary to our very survival. *Change is humanity's best friend.* Ordinary leaders fight it, visionary leaders delight in it. The ancient philosopher Marcus Aurelius captured these sentiments splendidly when he said, 'Observe always that everything is the result of change, and get used to thinking that there is nothing Nature loves so well as to change existing forms and make new ones like them.' "

"You've transformed the way I view change, Julian. I never would have thought that change is governed by the laws of nature and that it is so central, not only to the success of our company but to the progress of our society. Any other lessons on managing change?"

"One just hopped by," he replied, pointing to a frog with brown spots dotting its dark green back. "My little friend over here is a perfect example of what can happen to you if you decide to wait for large-scale changes to occur in your environment before you make the transition to the new pathways of thought and action that will help you survive."

"How so?"

"Well, if you take a frog and pop it into a pot of boiling water, what do you think will happen?"

"I'd bet it will try to jump out."

"Correct. Now let me offer you a different scenario. Let's say we started the frog off in water that was at room temperature and quietly let him relax in it. Then we gradually started turning up the heat until the water became hotter and hotter. What do you think would happen?"

"Don't tell me the frog would just sit there and do nothing?"

"It sure would, like most organizations do when the change creeping up on them is so incremental that it is easy to ignore. You see, like most companies, the internal system of the frog is only geared to respond and adapt to sudden environmental changes. So when slow changes like the gradual boiling of the water occur, it fails to react. It actually seems to enjoy itself. Then, when it least expects it, it boils to death, yet another casualty of a complacent mind-set."

"Great metaphor, Julian. When did you learn so much about biology?"

"I once dated a high school teacher who taught all that kind of stuff. At the time I found it boring, but now I realize that the laws of nature are essentially the laws of life. And the sooner we come to understand them and apply them in our daily lives, the sooner we will be able to use the changes that are pervading society to our own advantage. Remember, either you align yourself with the laws of nature or you'll find yourself against them."

"And boiled like our friend the frog," I added.

"You got it."

"What else can we do to manage change? I love the lessons you are sharing, Julian. They make so much sense."

"The leadership laws I've revealed to you this morning are all common sense. But most people are just too busy to discover them."

"So true."

"Next, I recommend that you encourage *your employees to become massively competent,*" came the quick reply. "It sort of relates to what I was just saying about being a lifelong learner. But it is even more than that. Being massively competent as an employee means that you stop waiting for management to hold your hand and guide you through the change process. Instead, you assume responsibility for yourself and situations that arise. If there are problems in your division, start thinking about ways that

next to my reading glasses. It was made of wood and had been given to me by Julian, just before I left him alone at the military base. It was the next piece of the intricate puzzle that had grown over the time we had been meeting. Once again, I could not make out the lightly colored design on it. And once again, it carried an inscription. It read simply, *Ritual 6: Leader Lead Thyself.*

The Ritual

Focus on the Worthy™

he Essence

The Ritual of Personal Effectiveness

he Wisdom

• The secret of personal effectiveness is concentration of purpose
• The art of getting things done lies in knowing what things need to remain undone
• If you do not lead your time, it will lead you
• If your priorities do not get scheduled into your planner, other peoples' priorities will get scheduled into your planner

he Practices

• The Time Model for Visionary Leadership™
• Strategic Time Blocking™

Quotable Quote

Never forget the importance of each and every one of your days. As you live your days, so you live your life. Do not waste even one of them. The past is history and the future is but a figment. This day, the present, is really all you have.

The Monk Who Sold His Ferrari

RITUAL 6

Leader Lead Thyself

꧁꧂

CHAPTER TEN

The Ritual of Self-Leadership

There is nothing noble in being superior to others.
True nobility lies in being superior to your former self.

Ancient Indian proverb

Mount Percival is the tallest peak in this part of the country. Mountaineers and adventurers come from far and wide to scale its north face, apparently one of the most treacherous of all of the climbs in our locale. A few years ago, the son of one of my colleagues lost his life on a summit attempt. He and the seven members of his team had been found frozen to death, about two hundred feet from the top. For the life of me, I could not figure out why Julian wanted me to meet him here.

As I drove my four-wheel drive up the winding highway that led to an area near the base of the mountain frequented by tourists and hikers, I realized I had come to rely on Julian's regular coaching sessions. Every single one of our meetings had not only been rich with leadership wisdom and powerful lessons on organizational transformation, they had also been mini-adventures that moved me out of my "region of security," to borrow from Julian's language, and into new pathways of thought and action. I sensed that he would not remain in one place for a very long time since I knew he was deeply committed to spreading the philosophy of the sages throughout our part of the world. And I knew that when he left, I would miss him.

As I drove up to the base area, crowded with people from all across the world on this fine day, I spotted Julian. Unlike the last time, today he had on his traditional ruby red monk's robe and his well-worn sandals. As usual, his face radiated vitality and good health. And as on each of the previous occasions, it carried a smile. It was still a little hard for me to believe that this youthful-looking man was actually Julian Mantle, the once hard-drinking, fast-living corporate player who had collapsed from a massive heart attack in the middle of a packed courtroom.

"Greetings, Peter!" Julian said with his usual degree of enthusiasm. "It's quite a day up here on the mountain," he added, taking a whiff of fresh air deep into his lungs. "Kind of makes me feel as if I was back in the Himalayas with Yogi Raman and the rest of my wise teachers."

"Do you miss their company?"

"Terribly. They were the kindest, most giving men and women I have ever known. They treated me like I was a part of their small family and I felt like they were a part of mine. Those days, up in that natural oasis of beauty, peace and knowledge were truly the best of my life. Having said that, I made a promise to them and I plan to keep it. I have a duty to perform and will dedicate the rest of my days to spreading their ideas about leadership in business and in life, making sure that their timeless message is heard by all those who need to hear it."

"Mind if I ask another question?"

"Not at all," Julian replied as we walked to the lodge to purchase a ticket up the mountain by cable car.

"Why are we going up there?" I asked as I strained my neck to look up at the summit.

"Because there is another leadership lesson I wish to share with you. And that is the perfect place for me to share it."

As we rode up the mountain, neither of us said a word. The beauty of the scenery was simply breathtaking, something to be taken in fully — and silently. With the feeling of joy that came over me through this connection to the gifts of nature, I wondered why I did not leave that oak-paneled office of mine more often to get outdoors and enjoy the simple pleasures of life. At least, I could bring Samantha and the kids up here on weekends. I really needed to spend more time with them. And I knew that such an outing would bring a greater sense of perspective to my days along with energy to my weeks.

After about half an hour of steady climbing, the cable car stopped abruptly and a voice on the public address system asked us to "de-car," a term I had never heard before and prayed I wouldn't again. Julian, obviously familiar with the place, led me along a snow-covered walkway lined on both sides with thick strands of rope. I silently followed my friend, placing my full trust in this man, who I had learned had my best interests in mind. Finally we arrived at our destination. And it was like nothing I had ever seen.

The ridge we were standing on looked out across the entire region as well as over other smaller mountains, which struggled to push through the billowy clouds in the otherwise clear blue sky. I truly wished Samantha and the kids were there with me. This sight would have amazed them. I felt deeply peaceful in this heavenly place and shared this sentiment with my youthful companion.

"I know what you mean, my friend. I know what you mean."

After a few minutes of soaking in the view, Julian began his lesson.

"Ritual 6 is an extremely important one, Peter, one that visionary leaders practice on a daily basis. If they fail to do so, even for a few days, their vision is diminished and much of their effectiveness is lost."

"Exactly what does Leader Lead Thyself mean?" I asked as I pulled the sixth piece of the puzzle from the light ski jacket I had put on for the occasion and glanced more closely at it.

"Ritual 6 is the ritual of self-leadership. Sadly, self-leadership is the discipline most neglected by leaders in this part of the world. And yet, it is the foundation from which all other success in business and in life springs."

"Is self-leadership the same as self-improvement?"

"It's about so much more than that. Sir Edmund Hillary, who as you know was the first person to reach the summit of Mount Everest, said it best when he observed, 'It is not the mountain we conquer but ourselves.' That's really the essence of self-leadership — it's about conquering and mastering yourself."

"Interesting."

"Most leaders believe that effectiveness and excellence come from external factors like an efficient work force or application of the latest technology. The truth of the matter, as visionary leaders have known over the centuries, is that success is an inside job. Excellence begins within. Market leadership begins with self-leadership."

After inhaling another deep breath of the crisp mountain air, Julian continued. "You see, Peter, how can you lead an organization if you've never learned how to lead yourself? How can you coach a team if you've never mastered the art of self-coaching? And how can you expect to manage others if you've never refined the skill of managing yourself?"

"My dad used to say that you can't do good if you don't feel good."

"Precisely. And Goethe made the point in a similar way when he noted that 'Before you can do something you must *be* something.' You cannot be the inspirational leader you hope to be if you wake up every morning feeling miserable and depressed. You cannot guide your people forward to victory if you are being kept behind by a lack of energy. You will not be able to capture their hearts and energize their minds if you are still yelling and screaming at them all day. Remember, before you can like another person, you must like yourself. *Success on the outside begins within.*

"It's like that old story my favorite professor told me when I was in law school," Julian added. "One night a father was relaxing with his newspaper after a long day at the office. His son, who wanted to play, kept on pestering him. Finally, fed up, the father ripped out a picture of the globe that was in the paper and tore it into many tiny pieces. 'Here, son, go ahead and try to put this back together,' he said, hoping this would keep the little boy busy long enough for him to finish reading his paper. To his amazement, his son returned after only one minute with the globe perfectly reassembled. When the startled father asked how he achieved this feat, the child smiled gently and replied, 'Dad, on the other side of the globe there was a picture of a person, and once I got the person together, the world was okay.' "

"So the lesson is that success on the outside really does begin within. It all starts by getting myself together. And once I do, my own world will be okay, correct?"

"Yes, Peter, that's it exactly."

"Are you suggesting that I make personal mastery one of my major goals?"

"Make it a vow."

"What's the difference?"

"A goal is something you aim to do, a positive intention that you plan to achieve sometime in the future. I discovered from the sages that a vow is something much deeper than that. Making a vow means you are committed, from the very core of your character, to keeping the promise you have made. Failure is simply not an option. By making a vow, you simply refuse to lose."

"Self-leadership is really that important?"

"Definitely. All the great thinkers have known of this truth. Seneca said, 'To master one's self is the greatest mastery,' while Confucius noted that 'good people strengthen themselves cease-lessly.' 'Man is made and unmade by himself,' discovered James Allen, while the sixth-century Chinese military leader Sun Tzu said, 'To secure ourselves against defeat lies in our own hands.' Even the modern leadership philosopher Peter Drucker observed that 'Self-development of the effective executive is central to the development of the organization, whether it be a business, a government agency, a research laboratory, a hospital or a military service. It is the way toward performance of the organization.'

"You see, my friend, one of the most enduring of all the ancient laws of humanity is that *we see the world not as it is, but as we are.* By improving, refining and defining who we are, we see the world from the highest, most enlightened perspective. By mastering ourselves, we see the world and all its limitless opportunities and potential from the top of the mountain rather than from the bottom. Commit yourself to excellence. Raise the personal standards you have set for yourself. Strive to do everything spectacularly well. *Remember that when you settle for mediocrity in the small things, you will also begin to settle for mediocrity in the big things. And anything less than a conscious commitment to peak personal performance is an unconscious commitment to weak personal performance.*

As I absorbed this profound piece of leadership wisdom, I gazed off into the horizon. I had never taken the time to think about self-improvement. I had often seen other executives reading personal development books, such as *As a Man Thinketh, University of Success, Think and Grow Rich, Psycho-Cybernetics* and *MegaLiving,* on my frequent airline flights and thought silently, 'There but for the grace of God go I,' assuming that these were poor souls suffering a professional or a personal crisis. I now realized that while those who could effectively manage others were wise, those who had mastered themselves were enlightened. The most important thing any leader could do to improve his organization was to first improve himself. My dad was right. You can't do good if you don't feel good. It is impossible to do great things if you are not thinking great thoughts. I had to make a "vow," as Julian suggested, to get serious about the development of my self so I could achieve all the things I wanted to achieve. I had to Focus on the Worthy and make the time to lift my inner life to a whole new level of effectiveness.

"Now do you see why I brought you up to the top of this mountain? To gain leadership over others, you must gain true leadership over yourself," Julian said. "You must climb your own mountains and rise to the top, conquering yourself in the process. You must stop making excuses for why things have gone wrong and assume some responsibility for a change. Visionary leaders are alibi-free."

"What do you mean by alibi-free?" I queried.

"As a litigation lawyer, I had the opportunity to cross-examine thousands of witnesses over the course of my career. No matter how guilty they were, they all did the same thing. They all came up with an excuse that shifted the blame to someone else. Not once could they clearly and simply admit, 'It was all my fault. I was wrong. And I am truly sorry.' "

"They all had alibis."

"Right. But visionary leaders are the masters of themselves, as well as of their destinies. They know that if there is a problem with morale in the company, there is a problem with their leadership. They understand that if their relationships are lacking in depth and warmth, there must be some lack within themselves. They know that if their levels of personal achievement are less than outstanding, the thoughts they are having and the actions they are taking must be less than superb. That's why I say that visionary leaders are alibi-free. They have the power of character to realize that they ultimately control their futures and that their outer lives are shaped by their inner ones.

"And just like scaling any great mountain," added Julian enthusiastically, "the higher you climb within yourself, the more you will see. The more you come to know who and what you really are as a person, performer and as a leader, the more value you will be able to contribute to the world around you. The saddest thing I know of is a human being who has no sense of self, no idea of what she could achieve in her life if only she had the courage to liberate her full potential through the discipline of self-mastery. Too many people live far below their potential. It's like Wordsworth once wrote, 'The world is too much with us; late and soon,/ Getting and spending, we lay waste our powers:/ Little we see in nature that is ours;/ We have given our hearts away, a sordid boon!' The point I'm really trying to make can be made very simply: *Leadership in your world begins with leadership of your life.*"

Julian then walked over to a long wooden bench that rested along the ridge and sat down. Closing his eyes and again deeply breathing in the cool, clean air of this spectacular mountain hide-away, he paused before continuing his passionate discourse on the value of self-leadership.

"You know, Peter, I really love this place. Since I've returned from the Himalayas, I've probably been up here fifty times. It really keeps my head clear. Life with the sages was so serene and peaceful. While they were enormously productive people, their achievement was of a graceful sort. Now that I'm back, I have to admit that I must constantly try not to get swept up in the frenetic pace that dogs our society."

"I feel the same way," I replied. "I mean the pace that I keep at the office is crazy. I'm like a wild man most days. Did you know that my executive assistant, Arielle, has already organized my appointment schedule for the next thirteen months? The number of people I have to see and the amount of work I have to do is absolutely unbelievable. Though the Time Model for Visionary Leadership that you shared with me is beginning to free me to Focus on the Worthy, I still feel the stress."

"Which brings me nicely to the first of the 5 Ancient Disciplines for Self-Leadership. These disciplines are formula-tions of the timeless wisdom that Yogi Raman gave me for personal mastery. Best practices for human excellence and inner leadership, if you will. Yogi Raman saw that I was in pretty bad shape when I arrived in the Himalayas, still recovering from my heart attack. So he offered me a series of philosophies and techniques to get my internal world back into shape. Let me simply say that the changes that followed when I applied these strategies were profound. The sense of tranquility that I had lost as a corporate superstar returned. I was able to conquer the worry habit that had plagued me for so long. My energy levels soared. I began to feel the way I had as an idealistic kid at Harvard Law School. And I knocked many years off the way I looked."

"No kidding," I observed with a smile. "I thought you were some kid when I saw you standing in my rose garden that day. Your transformation is astonishing. I'd love to hear how you did it. What's the First Discipline for Self-Leadership?"

"It's the Discipline of Personal Renewal. All visionary leaders regularly renew themselves. They make time to revitalize their bodies and energize their spirits. You see, in these information-crazed times that we live in, leaders and managers are being driven to do more with less, to work smarter, faster and harder. This frenetic pace that you are required to maintain just to keep up with the competition takes its toll on the way you think, feel and perform. But the thing you need to remember is that it's not really the stress that diminishes your effectiveness and leaves you feeling utterly exhausted at the end of the day."

"It's not?"

"No. What really does the damage is the failure of most leaders and managers to gain some *relief* from the inevitable stresses they face. As I told you earlier, some anxiety is always associated with change and change is the dominant force in business today. To thrive in this new economy, you have to work harder and aim higher. But virtues can become vices when practiced to excess, and overwork needs to be balanced with downtime. The best way to do this is to get regular relief through self-renewal activities. As the Chinese philosopher Lao Tzu said, 'All action begins in rest. That is the ultimate truth.' This will make you stress-hardy and allow you to maintain high levels of stamina and creativity for longer periods of time. I suggest you make a weekly sabbatical a top priority."

"What's a weekly sabbatical?"

"In the old days, people were required to observe a day of rest at the end of each working week. This day, known as the Sabbath, was used to relax, connect with family, enjoy personal hobbies or pursue spiritual activities. As a result, workers would begin the new week full of energy, zeal and conviction, ready to face the challenges their jobs would inevitably provide. Sadly, this tradition has been passed over, for most people and hard-driving executives believe that nonstop work routines are the only way to get to the top. It is only when they are afflicted with ulcers, migraines and early heart attacks that they wake up and begin to change the way they work and live. Unfortunately, by then it is sometimes too late. Believe me, my friend, I'm speaking from personal experience.

"So what I'm suggesting," continued Julian, "is that you designate a period every single week for some serious personal renewal. Time spent recharging your batteries is never a waste but a necessary aspect of any peak performance routine. Recreation is about re-creation. Time spent on genuine recreation makes you stronger, smarter and a better leader. Abe Lincoln captured the essence of what I am saying when he remarked, 'If I had eight hours to chop down a tree, I'd spend six hours sharpening my axe.' "

"So what you are saying is that working the way I do, without ever taking a vacation or even a regular day off to unwind, is the same as driving my BMW full-out, day after day without ever taking the time for a pit stop."

"Right. *Failing to devote time to the discipline of self-renewal is like saying you are so busy driving that you don't have time to stop for gas.* Not the smartest way to think, is it?"

"I agree. But how can I make time for myself?"

"I've already given you the secret."

"Really?"

"Use the Time Model for Visionary Leadership and the technique of strategic time blocking that I shared with you when we were at the military base. During your Sunday night planning practice, which I know you have begun to ritualize, block out a period over the coming week for recreation, relaxation and the renewal that you need to perform at your best. Make sure that at least one of your weekly wins revolves around quiet time. And plan to invest at least one hour on your weekly sabbatical. It will return huge dividends to you over the long run, especially when it comes to effective thinking and problem solving in your work as a leader."

"Seriously?"

"Sure, Descartes made many of his most important intellectual discoveries while relaxing in bed, and Newton formulated the laws of gravity while meditating under an apple tree. Archimedes stumbled upon the laws of hydrostatics while soaking in a hot bath and Mozart composed one of his most famous pieces over a game of billiards. Even the sewing machine came about through an act of renewal."

"Really?"

"Elias Howe, a Massachusetts instrument maker, was deep in sleep when he had a bizarre dream. In it, he was being chased by

RITUAL 8

❦

Link Leadership to Legacy

CHAPTER TWELVE

The Ritual of Contribution and Significance

I cannot believe that the purpose of life is to be "Happy." I think the purpose of life is to be useful, to be responsible, to be compassionate. It is, above all, to matter: to count, to stand for something, to have made some difference that you have lived at all.

Leo C. Rosten

It was just before midnight when I drove up the long winding road that led to the observatory. Located out in the country, it usually sat empty except for the two astronomers who used it as their research base. I quickly parked my car and rushed up the stairs that would lead me into the main hall where Julian had instructed me to meet him promptly. The night was a spectacular one, with not a cloud in the sky. Even to the naked eye, the heavens were alight with the moon and the stars. I knew Julian would be pleased.

"Hi, Peter," Julian mumbled as he offered me a quick welcome before returning his concentration to the sights he had been observing through the massive telescope. "Glad that you could make it."

"I wouldn't have missed it for anything, my friend. Is there something in particular that we are looking for tonight?"

"Oh, yes. Tonight will be a very special evening. That I can promise you," he replied, not taking his eyes away from the telescope.

"You'll be happy to hear that, with the last piece of the puzzle you gave me, I finally got the whole thing together."

"And what did you discover?"

"Well, every time you gave me a new piece with one of the eight rituals carved into it, I could also detect some form of design on it. But I was never able to quite figure out what it was. As the pieces came together, I could see it was turning into a symbol of some sort, but without the last piece, I still couldn't tell what it was."

"And now do you know?"

"It's a star."

"Not just a star, my friend. It's *the* star."

"I'm not sure that I follow you, Julian."

"Every star in the moonlit sky is bright. But one star in particular is brilliant."

"Which one's that?"

"It is the North Star, the most luminescent of them all."

Suddenly Julian let out a yell. "There it is! It's time! Let's go," he cried, leading me by the arm as he ran out of the building. We raced down the steps and along a winding path that led us into a vast field. Then we stopped and just stood there in silence.

"It's happening just like the sages promised it would," remarked Julian with delight.

"What's happening?" I asked, not observing anything out of the ordinary.

"This," he said, as he pointed up to a star that was beginning to flicker against the rich black coat of darkness that had dominated the evening sky. Growing brighter and brighter, its light started to flood the dark summer sky. Soon the star became so bright that I had to raise my hand in an effort to shield my eyes. It was a little like what had happened the night of the basketball game but a hundred times more intense. Before long, the entire sky was filled with light and it appeared as if it was the middle of the day, even though the dial on my watch indicated that it was a quarter past midnight. It was an unbelievable sight.

Looking over at Julian, I saw that he was beaming, his face full of joy and excitement. A radiant smile appeared on his youthful face and his hands were clasped together in the traditional way that the citizens of India greeted those they respected.

"Savor what you are seeing, Peter. The world won't see anything like this for another thousand years. The sages, in their infinite wisdom, had known this astronomical event would take place on this very night at this very time. I'm sure they must be experiencing it now, high up in their part of the world, just as we are witnessing it now in ours. I hope they're as moved by it as I am. I sure do miss them."

"What's this all about?" I asked, quickly looking back up at the sky before I lost another second.

"This, my friend, is nature's way of bringing in the dawn of a new era, a new age of leadership and life. There has been so much turmoil and turbulence in the world that many good people are giving up hope. They are losing faith in their power to make a difference. They are giving in to the demands of uncertainty and negativity, rather than transcending them and moving on to higher places of achievement, contribution and success. Many people in our society are even giving up on the gift of living. The natural phenomenon we're witnessing will act as a torchlight to remind leaders of their obligation to be visionaries. It will serve as their wake-up call to be the forces of good they are meant to be, illuminating their organizations just as the North Star has illuminated the sky on this very special night. Be a light, Peter. Be the one people look up to for guidance and direction. Let the ideal you aspire to burn brightly within you, blazing a path for all to see. This is your ultimate purpose in leadership — and in life."

Just as Julian had delivered this profound piece of wisdom, the night returned to its normal condition. We sat on the grass, Julian's robe growing creased and wrinkled. Then he continued, "One of the most timeless of all of the leadership laws is this one: *The Purpose of Life Is a Life of Purpose.*"

"Powerful statement."

"The greatest irony of leadership is that the more you give, the more you get. And when all is said and done, the highest and most enduring gift that you will ever be able to give is the gift of what you leave behind. Your legacy to the generations that follow will be how much value you have added to your organization and how many lives you have improved. As the great humanitarian Albert Schweitzer observed, 'There is no higher religion than human service. To work for the common good is the greatest creed.' Or perhaps even more to the point, let me use the words one father offered to his son while he lay on his deathbed, 'Be ashamed to die until you have scored a victory for mankind.' "

"So you're saying that visionary leaders, in practicing Ritual 8, link what they do with who they will serve."

"Nicely put, Peter. And in constantly focusing on leaving a rich footprint of service and contribution behind them when they depart, *such leaders link leadership to legacy.* In doing so, they fulfill their calling. They fulfill their duty to liberate the fullness of their personal gifts for a worthy cause. All the great leaders who have gone before us have aspired to reach this pinnacle, whether they were leaders in business, the sciences or even the arts. Just before his death, George Bernard Shaw was asked what he would do if he could live his life again. Though he had already achieved more in his lifetime than most of us could only dream of, he replied humbly, 'I would want to be the person I could have been but was not.'"

"Wise words," I replied.

"They are. They make me think of a short story penned by Leo Tolstoy called 'The Death of Ivan Ilych.' Ever read it?"

"No, Julian. To be honest I've never read any of Tolstoy's works. I guess I've never got around to it."

"There's such wisdom in the great books of literature and yet most people seem to be too busy to discover it. And so they continue to make mistakes both in their leadership and in their lives, mistakes that could so easily have been prevented had they taken a few hours out of their weeks to read deeply. In this particular story, Tolstoy wrote about Ivan Ilych, a vain, highly materialistic social climber who was more concerned about appearing successful than doing right. As a young man, he married, not because he loved and cherished his wife, but because high society approved of the match. He then had a number of kids, not because he wanted to have children but because that was what was expected of him. Rather than spending time with his family and building a rich home life, he devoted almost all his time to his work, becoming obsessed with his public persona as a top-level government lawyer.

"Soon, in an effort to keep up appearances, he began to live beyond his means, and eventually faced enormous financial hardship. This led to deep unhappiness and despair. As luck would have it, just when things were at their worst, he was offered a more prestigious and much higher-paying position as a judge. With his newfound good fortune, he bought the house of his dreams. He felt very proud of it and began to devote much of his time to furnishing the home with expensive antiques and fashionable furniture. The house had to be perfect, so all those around him would be suitably impressed.

"One day, when he was climbing a stepladder to show an upholsterer how he wanted a set of draperies hung, he fell and hurt his side. After the fall, he felt different and grew ill-tempered, often lashing out at his wife for the smallest transgression. A visit to a doctor revealed that he was seriously ill and various treatments were prescribed. But Ivan Ilych's condition only worsened. Within months, the once vital and jovial man appeared to be dying, his eyes lacking any expression of life and his body growing terribly weak. In his quiet agony, Ivan Ilych began to reflect on his life. First he thought about his childhood, then about his days as a striving adult and finally he contemplated the sad state he found himself in. Suddenly a question flooded his consciousness. A question that penetrated the deepest core of his being."

"What was it?"

"He asked himself this: *'What if my whole life has really been wrong?'* You see, Peter, for the first time in his life, he realized that all his jockeying for social position, all the energy he spent trying to look good and to be seen with the right people at the right events, was really not important. This dying man realized that life is a gift. And his could have been so much more than he had made of it. He could have contributed immensely and served greatly. He could have risked, dared and dreamed. He could have been the person he should have been. Instead, he squandered his days on frivolous matters of little consequence, matters that did nothing to improve the world around him. With that realization, his physical pain grew even worse and his mental torment became unbearable. He began to scream, and continued to do so for three full days.

"Then just two hours before his death," continued Julian, "he said to himself, 'Yes, it was all not the right thing.' He then grew silent and wondered, 'But what *is* the right thing?' Just then his young son, a schoolboy who had been deeply saddened by his father's illness, crept softly into the room and stood beside his bed. His father put a frail hand on the boy's head as the child began to cry. At that moment, a timeless truth was revealed to Ivan Ilych, one that most people never discover. He realized that though he had not lived his life as he should have lived, *it was still not too late to rectify his failure.* He realized that his duty was to serve all those around him and to enrich their lives in any way possible. He understood that the purpose of life was to make a difference through one's presence. If even one life was left a little better, it would have been worth living. So as his final act, he requested that his son leave the room so he would not have to endure any more of his father's suffering. He then closed his eyes and died."

I was deeply moved by this story. The power of the message Julian had just shared was not lost on me. I looked up at the sky, breathing in the fresh air and staring at nature's abundance. I reflected on all the time that had passed in my life and on all the things I had missed. I thought about the many men and women who counted on me and considered the duty I owed to them. I thought about the enormous potential of our company and regretted all the opportunities we had neglected. My thoughts then turned to my family. A lump came to my throat when I considered all of those special times I had missed with my two young sons. Little-league baseball games, Christmas concerts, sun-filled afternoons laughing in the park were all missed because I had not had the courage to spend my life well. I thought of my youngest son whose only request of me was to play and laugh a little more with him. I thought about his elder brother whom I had not spent even one quiet evening with in many months. I thought about Samantha and all the romantic getaways that I had promised we would go on, but never did. I really had missed out on living the life I was meant to live.

But, as Ivan Ilych came to appreciate, it was never too late to do what is right and live life fully. That moment I vowed to change the very person I was. I would become the kind of leader my heart told me I was capable of being. I promised myself I would be the kind of husband and father I knew I had the capacity to become. And I would live with the kind of soaring intensity I knew I deserved. At that moment, I looked over at Julian. Tears filled his eyes as well.

"I think you now understand what I've been saying, my friend. To be the kind of person that you are destined to be and to leave something special behind for all those who follow you is what life's all about. It is the essence of leaving a legacy. As Yogi Raman put it, '*What makes greatness is beginning something that does not end with you.*' "

"You know, Julian," I said as I wiped my eyes, "my dad used to say that 'the first fifty years of life are spent building one's legitimacy while the last fifty are to be devoted to building one's legacy.' I never quite understood what he meant until now."

"The sages had a saying that captures the essence of the point that your father in all his wisdom was trying to make."

"What was it?"

"They used to tell me that 'when you were born, the world rejoiced while you cried. Your mission must be to live your life in such a way that when you die, the world cries while you rejoice.' Only then will your life have made the difference it was intended to make."

"Just so I am perfectly clear, Julian, will my legacy then be the goals that I will have achieved over my life as a leader?"

"Your legacy must be so much more than that. Your legacy will ultimately be a manifestation of the deepest and the best that you had to give in life. It will be a reflection of the person you now are and the person you aim to be. Leaving a legacy is not about impressing your friends or reaching the top. It's not about looking good but about doing good. It's more about fulfilling your duty and actualizing your humanity. Legacy-Based Leadership is the most powerful type of leadership. Practicing it will allow you to do what few leaders in the world today can do."

"Which is?"

"*To create a successful present while building a brilliant future.* And if I may say so, Peter, every leader in every field of endeavor should aspire to no less."

Julian then walked me back to the entrance of the observatory. Under the steps was a little wooden box that had been covered by a clean white cloth. Julian reached down and picked the box up, carefully making sure that the precious contents were given their due respect.

"Here, this is for you. The time has finally come for me to leave and for you to explore the full magnificence of the 8 Rituals of Visionary Leaders on your own. I could not have asked for a better student and a more receptive friend. From the day I first exposed you to the leadership wisdom of the sages at our golf club, to this evening here at the observatory, you have embraced what I have come to share with an open mind and an honest heart.

"And so, as a token of my thanks for allowing me to fulfill my promise to Yogi Raman and spread the lessons I learned throughout our part of the world, I humbly offer you this gift. It has great meaning to me and has been my constant companion since I left the Himalayas. I couldn't think of a better home for it than with you. All I ask is that you sincerely continue to apply the knowledge that I have delivered to you and spread The 8 Rituals of Visionary Leaders throughout your organization for all to discover. In this way, not only will you transform your leadership, you will bless the lives of all those around you."

And with those final words, Julian reached over and embraced me as only a dear friend could, then dashed off into the darkness, his richly embroidered robe trailing behind him. As I opened the box, I saw that the gift was beautifully wrapped in some type of homemade covering. I immediately removed it, eager to find the special present Julian had placed within.

As I looked deeper, I saw that the box held a shiny object. A smile came to my face as I recognized what it was. It was the small telescope that Julian had been clinging to the night of the basketball game. I could not believe that he would have parted with such a prized possession. I knew how much his stargazing had meant to him.

Picking it up, I noticed that an inscription had been engraved on the telescope in elegant lettering. It said simply: *To my now wise friend, Peter, a man who I know will touch many lives. May your spark of leadership turn fear into power and darkness into light. With love, your fan, Julian.*

The Ritual	

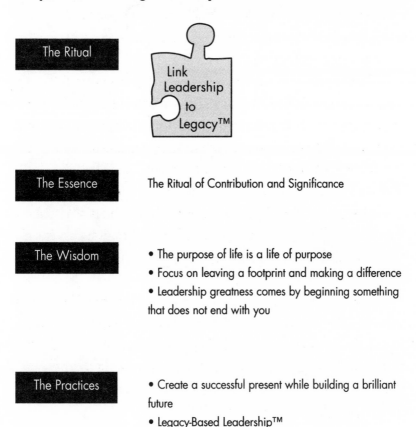

Link Leadership to Legacy™

The Essence	The Ritual of Contribution and Significance

The Wisdom

- The purpose of life is a life of purpose
- Focus on leaving a footprint and making a difference
- Leadership greatness comes by beginning something that does not end with you

The Practices

- Create a successful present while building a brilliant future
- Legacy-Based Leadership™

Quotable Quote

Your legacy will ultimately be a manifestation of the deepest and the best that you had to give in life. It will be a reflection of the person you now are and the person you aim to be. Leaving a legacy is not about impressing your friends or reaching the top. It's not about looking good but about doing good. It's about fulfilling your duty and actualizing your humanity.

The Monk Who Sold His Ferrari

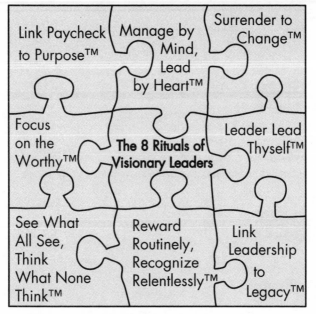

1. Link Paycheck to Purpose™
   (The Ritual of a Compelling Future Focus)

2. Manage by Mind, Lead by Heart™
   (The Ritual of Human Relations)

3. Reward Routinely, Recognize Relentlessly™
   (The Ritual of Team Unity)

4. Surrender to Change™
   (The Ritual of Adaptability and Change Management)

5. Focus on the Worthy™
   (The Ritual of Personal Effectiveness)

6. Leader Lead Thyself™
   (The Ritual of Self-Leadership)

7. See What All See, Think What None Think™
   (The Ritual of Creativity and Innovation)

8. Link Leadership to Legacy™
   (The Ritual of Contribution and Significance)

KEYNOTES & SEMINARS WITH
ROBIN S. SHARMA, LL.M.
Bestselling Author & Professional Speaker

Robin S. Sharma, LL.M., is one of North America's most dynamic, thought-provoking and energizing professional speakers. Each year, he travels more than 100,000 miles delivering his powerful wisdom on leadership, change, personal effectiveness and life management to major corporations, associations and educational institutions. His customized conference keynotes and in-house seminars are in constant demand by organizations seeking a high-content yet entertaining professional speaker who will provide immediately effective strategies to help their people reach all-new levels of productivity, performance and personal satisfaction.

Robin S. Sharma's current programs include:
- The 8 Rituals of Visionary Leaders™
- The Disciplines of Peak-Performing Managers™
- Strategic Time Leadership in the Digital Age™
- The Success Rituals of Top Sales Producers™
- Success Wisdom from The Monk Who Sold His Ferrari™
- How to Gain Leadership Over Your Life™
- Awakening Spirit and Character at Work

For a complete listing of Robin S. Sharma's seminars, best-selling books, audio products, high-profile clients and speaking schedule, visit the Sharma Leadership International website at **www.robinsharma.com.** He also provides personal coaching to a very select number of executives through his one-of-a-kind mentoring program.

To book Robin S. Sharma for your next conference or in-house event, please contact:
Shashi Tangri
National Program Director
Sharma Leadership International
7B Pleasant Boulevard, Suite 957
Toronto, Ontario
Canada M4T 1K2
Toll-Free: 1-888-RSHARMA (774-2762)
Facsimile: 905-780-0283
E-mail: wisdom@robinsharma.com
Website: www.robinsharma.com

THE SHARMA LEADERSHIP REPORT™

FREE subscription offer to purchasers of *Leadership Wisdom from The Monk Who Sold His Ferrari* for a limited time only. (Each issue has a $7.50 value.)

The Sharma Leadership Report, Robin S. Sharma's popular newsletter, is packed with practical wisdom, lessons and tips that you can apply immediately to improve the quality of your life. This highly inspirational report focuses on leading-edge topics for personal, professional and character development including self-esteem, strategic time management, peak performance, discipline, creativity, life-career balance, relationships, self-leadership, stress mastery and leadership renewal.

To order your free subscription, write to us at the address below or visit our website at **www.robinsharma.com**.

Free Subscription Offer
Sharma Leadership International
7B Pleasant Boulevard, Suite 957
Toronto, Ontario
Canada M4T 1K2
E-mail: wisdom@robinsharma.com

POWERFUL WISDOM FOR LEADERSHIP IN BUSINESS AND IN LIFE

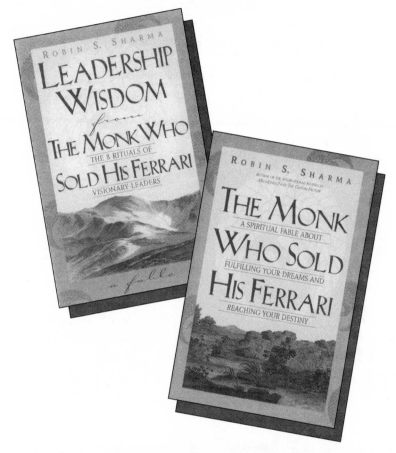

NOW AVAILABLE IN ALL GOOD BOOKSTORES.

Discounts available on quantity purchases for your organization. Please call 1-888-RSHARMA or e-mail wisdom@robinsharma.com for pricing information.

WE HAVE A REQUEST

Robin S. Sharma would love to hear how this book has affected both you and your organization. Share your success stories, insights and experiences. Do you have a tip or quotes that you would like to share with other readers in Robin's popular newsletter *The Sharma Leadership Report*™? Please send them to us. Robin will make every possible effort to respond with a personal note. We want to hear from you!

Please write to Robin S. Sharma c/o:

SHARMA LEADERSHIP INTERNATIONAL
7B Pleasant Blvd., Suite 957
Toronto, Ontario
Canada
M4T 1K2
E-mail: wisdom@robinsharma.com

ROBIN S. SHARMA ON THE WEB:
For the latest wisdom and thinking on professional
and personal leadership issues, visit the
Sharma Leadership International website
at www.robinsharma.com